The I Ching Oracle

A guide through the human maze

The I Ching Oracle

A guide through the human maze

Timothy and Johanna Dowdle

BOOKS

Winchester, UK
Washington, USA

JOHN HUNT PUBLISHING

First published by O-Books, 2021
O-Books is an imprint of John Hunt Publishing Ltd., 3 East St., Alresford,
Hampshire SO24 9EE, UK
office@jhpbooks.com
www.johnhuntpublishing.com
www.o-books.com

For distributor details and how to order please visit the 'Ordering' section on our website.

Design: Stuart Davies

UK: Printed and bound by CPI Group (UK) Ltd, Croydon, CR0 4YY
Printed in North America by CPI GPS partners

We operate a distinctive and ethical publishing philosophy in
all areas of our business, from our global network of authors to
production and worldwide distribution.

Contents

This book is dedicated to the memory of Richard Wilhelm (1873-1930) who brought the I Ching oracle to the West.

Preface

In times of crisis or uncertainty the *I Ching or Book of Changes* can serve as an oracle and a guide to help us deal successfully with the difficulties and challenges of life. The phenomenon of change is the most powerful force impacting on our lives. It can come suddenly and unexpectedly, sweeping aside our sense of security and leaving us struggling to cope with a drastically changed reality. Or, we may be unsatisfied with the way our lives are going and would like to make a change, but do not know how.

The reader can consult the I Ching oracle by simply asking it a question. It answers by pointing to a text which, amazingly accurately, applies to the situation the reader is experiencing. The oracle then goes on to advise the reader how to overcome any difficulties he/she is facing. However, the original I Ching text is written in a coded, metaphorical language that is difficult to understand.

The I Ching Oracle – A guide through the human maze is a modern interpretation of the I Ching oracle text, designed to help the reader find a way through the challenges and complexities of everyday life. It provides the reader with a road map, a detailed route description, to navigate a way through the human maze we find ourselves living in.

This book will show the reader how to consult the I Ching oracle and receive clear answers to any important questions. It will enable the reader to consult the oracle completely independently without needing assistance from anybody. Our book is intended to be a guide for all people of independent spirit who are following an individual path.

The I Ching Oracle – A guide through the human maze is based on our personal experience of consulting the oracle over a period of more than thirty years. We have personally been

1

through many of the changes the I Ching hexagrams represent. Our descriptions of the hexagrams are often autobiographical, but they can equally apply to everyone who is living through similar experiences. For example, our narrative of hexagram 56 *The Wanderer* is entirely autobiographical. For many years we have led a wandering life and have often received hexagram *The Wanderer* in an I Ching consultation. On those occasions we almost always had to make a long journey and eventually find a home in a different place.

Many books have been written about the I Ching, both in China and the West. The authors like to think of this body of knowledge as a structure, a kind of tower, to which every new publication adds a brick. As the knowledge grows and evolves, the tower grows in height and width, generation after generation. The authors would like to share the knowledge they have gleaned from consulting the I Ching oracle, and make a contribution to I Ching literature.

Our interpretation of the I Ching features *the Experiencer* as the central character, experiencing the changes described in the hexagrams. The reader is invited to follow in the footsteps of *the Experiencer* and anticipate how his/her present situation will change in the future.

Timothy and Johanna Dowdle
July 2020

Part I

Using The I Ching As An Oracle

Chapter 1

Introduction

1.1 What is the I Ching?

The I Ching or Book of Changes is an ancient Chinese book of divination. It is a unique collection of archetypal situations which are presented in a series of 64 hexagrams and 384 lines. An archetype is a template that can be continuously duplicated. Archetypal situations are experiences, continuously duplicated and repeated, shared by people all over the world. For example, in *Hexagram 5 Waiting for Nourishment* the I Ching uses the imagery of *waiting for the rain to come* to symbolize a universal experience of anxiously waiting for the benefits of nourishment.

In the original I Ching text every situation represented by the hexagrams and lines is assessed in short, sometimes terse, judgments, using a curious metaphorical language that is difficult to penetrate if one is unfamiliar with the cultural context. Each judgment describes a given situation *and the situation it will develop into*. In addition, the judgments give advice on how to act in these situations.

This book of timeless wisdom has an enduring relevance for all cultures and all times. It serves as an oracle and a guide for those who are following a path of personal development with the aim of achieving fulfillment. The I Ching represents a path of personal growth *through the experience of change*, because *change* is the engine of development. The experience of change leads to knowledge and this creates the potential to achieve fulfillment.

Consulting the I Ching oracle will help us to understand the reality of a situation, its deeper meaning and the implications for the future. The oracle will give the reader invaluable advice on how to deal with any given situation. It will give crucial information about the reader's current situation and predict any changes that will occur. Consulting the oracle on a regular basis will help the reader to find a way through the changes in his/her life and develop a strong sense of purpose.

1.2 Our relationship with the I Ching

We have been consulting the I Ching for thirty years, keeping a detailed record of all the questions we asked and all the answers we received. Building up our knowledge of the I Ching has been a long and gradual learning process. When we first began consulting the oracle, we did not always understand the answers to our questions; many of the descriptions of the hexagrams and lines were baffling. We had to rely on modern I Ching interpretations, but, unfortunately, a good deal of these commentaries proved to be inaccurate or misleading.

The only way we could gain a real understanding of the hexagrams was through personal experience. Whenever we consulted the oracle and received a hexagram we could not understand, we eventually learned the meaning of the hexagram simply by living through the experience the hexagram represents. Over time this empirical knowledge enabled us to penetrate into the meaning of the ancient Chinese judgments and make a comparative study of the hexagrams. As a result of this learning process our relationship with the Book of Changes has deepened and strengthened over the years.

In times when we were uncertain or confused we would ask the I Ching to shed its light on our difficulties and show us the way through. Time after time the I Ching described our experiences with amazing accuracy and gave tremendously good advice on how to deal with all kinds of situations. The I Ching always told us the truth, but sometimes the truth can be hard to accept.

The I Ching oracle separates illusion from reality, encouraging the reader to be realistic and come to terms with what is.

Coming to terms with the reality does not mean giving up on one's dreams or aspirations; it means following a path that is true and without illusions. This often involves going through a process of personal change. Awareness and self-honesty are essential to successfully undergo change and make progress.

Following the guidance of the I Ching has changed our lives in many ways, enabling us to make progress in areas we could never have imagined possible. We continue to consult the oracle whenever we have important questions, benefitting from its invaluable advice and predictions of future developments.

1.3 A brief history of the I Ching

The I Ching is one of the oldest books in the world, its origins dating back to ancient times (2000-1800 BCE). The art of divination was practiced in ancient China long before historical records began, and over the centuries diviners pieced together a system of trigrams to study the mechanism of change and predict the future. Later these trigrams were combined to form hexagrams. Traditional scholars have attributed King Wen (ca. 1000 BCE) and his son, the Duke of Chou, with authorship of the final compilation of the 64 hexagrams. Their work consists of a written text, known as *The Judgments and The Lines*. *The Judgments* give advice on how to respond, or deal with, the situations the hexagrams represent. *The Lines* give similar advice for the situations represented by the individual lines of the hexagrams. The entire text of *The Judgments and The Lines* is an extraordinary work and demonstrates a masterful knowledge of archetypal situations.

Since the time of King Wen several more layers of text have been added to the I Ching, most notably a series of brilliant commentaries on the judgments which can be directly attributed to Confucius (550-479 BCE) and the Confucian School. These commentaries clarify and expand on the work of King Wen and the Duke of Chou, providing an in-depth analysis of the hexagrams and the individual lines.

In the second century CE, Wang Bi (226-249) wrote an excellent interpretation of the I Ching which became influential in China for hundreds of years. His detailed analysis of the structure of the hexagrams opened up a new perspective on the meaning of each hexagram in terms of actual experience. By studying the interaction of the lines of a hexagram Wang Bi succeeded in defining and explaining the dynamic of a hexagram, and therefore the actual experience it represents.

During the Sung dynasty (960-1200) neo-Confucian scholars made major contributions to the I Ching, most notably Shao Yong (1011-1077) and Zhu Xi (1130-1200).

Shao Yong developed a mathematical model of change, based on the movement of Yin and Yang lines changing into their opposites. This model illustrates how the phenomenon of cyclic change manifests itself in the ever-recurring pattern of growth and decline. On the basis of his mathematical model of change Shao Yong designed a purely numerological method for consulting the oracle, known as the Plum Blossom Numbers.

Zhu Xi emphasized the importance of the I Ching as a book of divination and encouraged every citizen of the state to consult it. He declared that all of the people, including the common folk, can consult the I Ching to determine the path of good fortune and avoid misfortune. And very importantly, Zhu Xi rediscovered the original yarrow stalk method to consult the oracle, which is used to this day. Zhu Xi wrote a commentary, titled "Original Meaning of the Changes" and a handbook on divination, called "Introduction to the Study of the Changes". The reader can find a detailed description of the yarrow stalk method in chapter 2 of this book, sub 2.4.1 The stick method.

In 1715 the Kangxi Emperor (1662-1722) ordered an imperial edition of the I Ching to be compiled and published, which includes all of the important commentaries. This is by far the most comprehensive version of the I Ching ever produced.

In modern times the missionary and scholar Richard Wilhelm (1873-1930) translated the 1715 imperial edition into German under the title *I Ging, Das Buch der Wandlungen* (first published in Germany in 1924). This work was eventually translated into English by Cary Baynes, appearing in print in 1950 under the title *The I Ching or Book of Changes*.

Richard Wilhelm lived and worked in China for twenty years, becoming fluent in the language and gaining a firsthand knowledge of Chinese culture. He began working on his translation of the I Ching in 1913 in collaboration with a Chinese scholar, Lao Nai-hsüan. Despite many interruptions, including a major war, the translation work was completed nearly ten years later. This was a triumph and a deeply fulfilling experience for him.

Wilhelm saw the great significance of the I Ching, as both a book of divination and a guide through the changes and challenges of life. We advise all I Ching students to buy a copy of the Richard Wilhelm translation in order to read the translated Chinese judgments as a way to personally connect with the spirit of the I Ching.

We would also like to pay special tribute to William de Fancourt's work in tracing the history of the I Ching as described in his book *Warp and Weft* (see Bibliography). It is a very informative work, exploring in detail the history and the origins of the I Ching.

1.4 The mechanism of change

In this world the movement of opposites creates time. Opposites displace one another in a pattern that repeats itself again and again, producing cyclic change. For example, the cycle of day and night (light and darkness), the cycle of the seasons (hot and cold), the cycle of growth and decay, etc., etc. The movement of opposites also creates thought. High and low, hot and cold, near and far, all these words weave a pattern of thought based upon the movement of opposites. In this way the human mind mirrors the passage of time.

In the I Ching the passage of time can be observed in the movement of the opposing principles of Yin and Yang. A hexagram consists of six Yin and/or Yang lines. A Yin line is a broken line and a Yang line is a solid line. Yin and Yang lines displace one another in the same way that light displaces darkness and heat displaces cold. When a Yin line is displaced ("moves"), a Yang line appears and replaces it. Similarly, when a Yang line is displaced ("moves"), a Yin line appears and replaces it. This movement transforms one hexagram into another. (See for detailed explanation chapter 1.5 and chapter 3.1 of this book.) And when one hexagram is transformed into another, we can observe the movement of time from the present into the future. In this way the I Ching perfectly mirrors actual reality, because it uses the movement of opposites to reflect the mechanism of change. This is how the I Ching predicts the future.

1.5 Trigrams and Hexagrams

1.5.1 The Trigrams

The eight trigrams are the result of all possible combinations of three Yin and/or Yang lines.

Each trigram is unique and has its own special character. The I Ching uses phenomena from the world of nature to symbolize the essential meaning of each trigram, e.g. water flowing through a ravine, a mountain, an earthquake.

The Creative is pure creative energy and a force for the good.

It is also the power to endure. This trigram symbolizes **heaven**, a timeless place of radiant light and the source of all creative power.

The Receptive is the receptive mind, experiencing and responding to events. It cannot take the lead; it can only follow. This trigram symbolizes planet **Earth**, the vessel containing all living beings.

Keeping Still is the time when action has ceased and everything has come to a halt. It is also the time before action resumes again. This trigram pictures a **mountain** to symbolize a total lack of movement.

Flowing Water is the force to push through difficult situations. It also means danger. This trigram represents **flowing water** pushing through a narrow gorge and constantly in danger of becoming trapped.

The Shock is a sudden movement of action, of events suddenly gathering pace. It also means taking action or being on the receiving end of an action. This trigram is a symbol of a powerful **earthquake** and represents a sudden, disruptive movement or action.

Penetration is the slow process of learning and gathering information. It is also the power to penetrate into a situation and influence people. This trigram represents a gentle **wind**, penetrating into everything.

Clarity is the power of awareness that enables one to see a situation or one's fellow human beings clearly. This trigram symbolizes **fire** to represent the power of awareness in sentient beings.

The Joyful is paradoxical, because it means both happiness and sadness. It represents enthusiasm and the ability to communicate with others. Sadness comes when joy and enthusiasm cannot last. This trigram pictures a **mouth** to represent the expression of joy through speech.

1.5.2 The Hexagrams

A hexagram is a combination of two trigrams. All possible combinations of the eight trigrams produce in total 64 hexagrams. The interaction of the two primary trigrams in each hexagram creates the energy and the conditions characteristic of a specific situation. To illustrate how the interaction of two trigrams represents *an actual situation* in the form of a hexagram, the following three examples show a number of different combinations of trigrams.

Example 1

When trigrams *The Receptive* and *The Creative* are combined, hexagram *Peace* is formed.

Hexagram 11 *Peace*. The upper primary trigram is *The Receptive*; the lower primary trigram is *The Creative*.

Peace represents a time of happiness and prosperity. The energy of *The Creative* is flowing into the vessel of *The Receptive* and everything flourishes.

When hexagram *Peace* is reversed, hexagram *Standstill* is formed.

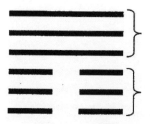

Hexagram 12 *Standstill*. The upper primary trigram is *The Creative*; the lower primary trigram is *The Receptive*.

Standstill represents a time of stagnation. The energy of *The Creative* is flowing out of the vessel of *The Receptive*. As a result nothing can thrive.

Example 2

When trigrams *Clarity* and *Flowing Water* are combined, hexagram *The Crossing* is formed.

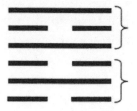

Hexagram 64 *The Crossing*. The upper primary trigram is *Clarity*; the lower primary trigram is *Flowing Water*.

The Crossing represents an all-out effort to make a major transition.

The lower primary trigram *Flowing Water* indicates danger. The Experiencer is at risk of making a wrong move and will have to tread carefully. The upper primary trigram *Clarity* means the Experiencer will have to gain a clearer sense of direction and purpose.

When hexagram *The Crossing* is reversed, hexagram *After the Crossing* is formed.

Hexagram 63 *After the Crossing*. The upper primary trigram is *Flowing Water*; the lower primary trigram is *Clarity*.

After the Crossing represents a time period after a successful transition has been accomplished. The Experiencer embarks on a new phase in life and achieves a good deal of success. However, this will not last, because over time the situation will go into decline and gradually become unsustainable.

The upper primary trigram *Flowing Water* indicates difficulties and danger ahead. The lower primary trigram *Clarity* shows the Experiencer has the clarity of mind to foresee the difficulties ahead and take the necessary measures in time.

Example 3

When the trigrams *Keeping Still* and *The Joyful* are combined, hexagram *Decrease* is formed.

Hexagram 41 *Decrease*. The upper primary trigram is *Keeping Still*; the lower primary trigram is *The Joyful*.

Decrease represents a time of severe limitations. The Experiencer has to cope with feelings of loss, sadness and frustration.

The upper primary trigram *Keeping Still* indicates the Experiencer's personal progress has ground to a halt in the current situation. The lower primary trigram *The Joyful* paradoxically represents sadness here, because the Experiencer's potential for joy and enthusiasm cannot find expression or release at this time.

When hexagram *Decrease* is reversed, hexagram *Influence* is formed.

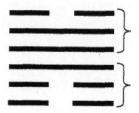

Hexagram 31 *Influence*. The upper primary trigram is *The Joyful*; the lower primary trigram is *Keeping Still*.

The lower primary trigram *Keeping Still* indicates the Experiencer is in a strong position, but will have to wait for the right opportunity to make a move. The upper primary trigram *The Joyful* represents the Experiencer's ability to communicate with others. The combination of these two trigrams means the Experiencer will be able to have a strong influence on people.

Chapter 2

How to consult the I Ching oracle

2.1 Questions to ask the I Ching

Over many years of consulting the I Ching we have found that formulating the right question is the only way to receive a clear and direct answer.

Straightforward and direct questions about issues relevant to the reader's own situation will receive the clearest answers from the I Ching. For example: "Should I look for a different job?" or "Should we buy this house?" Or, "How should I deal with the problems in my relationship?" or "Why do I have difficulties with my boss?" The reader will need to ask pertinent questions that involve making important decisions, following specific strategies or changing one's approach.

Composite questions, such as "Should I sell the house or put it up for rental?" or "Should I sell the house and move to another town?" will not receive a clear answer. The reader may instead receive a hexagram pointing out his/her indecisiveness or confusion. The solution is to split composite questions into single issue questions. For example, "Should I sell the house?" followed, if necessary, by "Should I put the house up for rental?"

If the reader is confronted with difficult choices or complicated issues, he/she may need to ask the I Ching a series of questions. In this case the I Ching will provide information and advice using several different hexagrams and moving lines. It is important to note that, although these hexagrams may appear to be completely different, they can often represent different aspects of the same situation.

The I Ching will not address purely hypothetical or unrealistic questions that have no bearing on the reality. If the reader asks the I Ching a question that has no relevance or validity because he/she is confused or stressed, it will not give a direct answer. Instead, the I Ching will provide relevant information about the reader's actual situation, in which case he/she may be baffled by the reply and wonder if the I Ching is actually answering the question. Under these circumstances it is very important to carefully study the information the I Ching is giving, because it will help to provide clarity and clear away confusion. The I Ching will help the reader to see the situation as it really is, which can be surprisingly or shockingly different from the reader's own impression.

2.2 Understanding how the oracle works

Consulting the I Ching is an extraordinary way to access knowledge about the past, present and future. However, the source of this knowledge is a mystery. Where does this information come from?

The authors believe that the source of this knowledge is innate and therefore resides in the subconscious. This means that whoever consults the I Ching will access knowledge from his/her subconscious.

The Greek philosopher Plato (427-347 BCE) has written an account of an afterlife experience in *The Republic*, under the title *The Myth of Er*. This is a riveting story of a warrior who died on the battlefield and passed away into the afterlife, but miraculously his body returned to life and he came back to tell the tale. The essence of the story is the eyewitness account of a dead warrior witnessing people watching their past and future lives unfold in a place beyond time and space, where past, present and future can be viewed simultaneously.

This story illustrates what an amazing phenomenon the human mind is; it records everything. All experiences are recorded and stored in the repository of memory. Furthermore, the mind not only records everything that occurs in the present, but has previously, prior to its current state of consciousness in its present incarnation, already recorded everything that will occur in the future. If this is true, the reader who consults the I Ching oracle will gain access to his/her innate knowledge of the future.

There is another mystery. The I Ching oracle also provides the reader with help and advice on whatever situation or predicament the reader is in. Where does this help come from? Who is advising the reader? There has long been, deep in the human psyche, a belief in guides and guardian angels from beyond this world who watch over us and guide us in times of difficulty. Is it possible that, when consulting the oracle, we are also contacting help from beyond? Wherever this advice comes from, it is uncannily accurate and helps the reader to face the changes he/she is going through.

However, it is not possible to determine *a time factor* for how long the prediction of the oracle will take to fulfill itself. This could support the theory that the source of the oracle is in a place beyond time and space, where past, present and future are collapsed into one dimension.

The I Ching oracle is consulted by using a random selection method, either by tossing coins or by randomly splitting bundles of sticks. It is essential to use a random selection method, because it opens a direct connection with the source of the oracle, bypassing the conscious intellect. It is the only way to access the source of the oracle; it cannot be directly accessed by the conscious mind.

Accessing this knowledge can be compared to using Morse code in radio communications, where speech cannot be used. The sender can use Morse code to send information which the receiver can decipher using a conversion table for Morse signals. The signals are received from left to right, as in Roman script, and then converted into letters. The I Ching also uses a code, but it is in the form of numbers obtained by tossing coins or manipulating bundles of sticks. These numbers are converted into the lines of a hexagram according to a predetermined system, in the same way that Morse signals are decoded using the Morse-conversion table.

Before starting the consultation the reader will need to decide whether to assemble the hexagram *from the top down* or *from the bottom up*. Traditionally, hexagrams are assembled from the bottom up in a consultation, because time progresses upward in a hexagram; the bottom line is the nearest to the present and the top line is the furthest away in the future.

However, the authors have always assembled hexagrams *from the top down* and this has consistently produced accurate results over a period of many years. Our understanding is that the source of the oracle presents information about the future in a chronological order from the furthest point away in time towards the present. For this reason we prefer to build a hexagram from the top, which is the furthest point away in the future, moving downward towards the present, perfectly duplicating the flow of information from the source.

Recent scientific research[1] about the functioning of the brain in relation to *time* seems to confirm our chosen method for assembling hexagrams. Experiments have shown that the human brain has the ability to know in advance what is yet to happen. Information about the future presents itself in the brain in reverse order; information about events furthest away in time manifests itself first, followed in chronological order by information about events closer to the present.

1. Source: Disc 1, What the Bleep!? Ultra-Extended Quantum Rabbit Hole Part One, section 10 "Time", and disc 4, Scientist Interviews Part One, interview with *Stuart Hameroff, MD*, "Time and Consciousness". DVD-

set *What the Bleep!? Down the Rabbit Hole, Quantum Edition,* Revolver Entertainment, London, UK, 2006.

2.3 Preparation for the consultation

There are a number of important points to keep in mind when preparing for a consultation.

- Have a clear question in mind and try to get as much clarity as possible about the current situation by doing factual research. The more the reader knows about the subject in question, the easier it will be to understand the I Ching's answer in the context of the actual situation.
- Choose a quiet moment and a quiet place to consult the oracle. Set aside enough time for the consultation, for example an evening without appointments, and choose a reasonably peaceful environment to minimize the risk of being disturbed by interruptions or noise.
- Choose a method for consulting the oracle, either sticks or coins, and set ready the implements. Use a notebook to record all questions put to the oracle and the answers received. This will prove invaluable for future reference and will help to build up one's personal experience with the oracle.
- Have an open mind and be prepared to accept the I Ching's answer, whatever it may be. This can be difficult if the reader is very dependent on a certain outcome. The oracle will tell the truth about a situation, like a wise uncle who will not give easy answers. Over time the reader will come to appreciate the I Ching as his/her best friend for its honest and reliable advice.
- To achieve a quiet and open mind we advise the reader to take a rest, meditate or pray for about 5 to 10 minutes before starting the actual consultation. It is important to be in "fully receptive mode" when performing the

consultation procedure; in this way the reader will be completely open to receive the message.

2.4 Choosing the method of consultation

There are two traditionally known methods for consulting the I Ching oracle, *the stick method* and *the coin method*. The coin method is faster and easier, but the stick method is more precise. The reason for this is that the stick method uses more random selection moments (i.e. more contact moments with the source of the oracle) than the coin method. In the stick method there is a random selection moment every time one splits the bundle of sticks, resulting in 3 moments per line and 6x3=18 moments per hexagram. In the coin method every toss of the coins is a random selection moment, resulting in one moment per line and 6x1=6 moments per hexagram.

2.4.1 The stick method

Fifty dried yarrow stalks approximately 8 inches (20 cm) long are traditionally used in an I Ching consultation. If these are not available, fifty wooden sticks, for example, barbecue skewers, or stalks of about the same length and thickness will serve the purpose. It is important that the sticks have never been used for other purposes; they should only be used for consulting the oracle.

The consultation starts by laying the bundle of 50 sticks on the table and randomly selecting one stick to be set aside for the duration of the consultation. The remaining 49 sticks will be used for the rest of the consultation. It takes three rounds of manipulating the sticks to obtain one line of a hexagram.

Round 1:

Pick up the bundle of 49 sticks and split it randomly into two bundles and lay those down on the table in two separate stacks. Take a stick from the right hand stack and put it between the ring finger and the little finger of the left hand. Pick up the left hand stack with the left hand and start counting off little bundles of four sticks with the right hand, putting them on the table, until four or less sticks are left in the left hand. Put the remaining sticks in the left hand between the ring finger and the middle finger of the left hand. Pick up the right hand stack, put it in the left hand, and perform the same procedure, counting off little bundles of four sticks until four or less sticks are left. Put these remaining sticks between the middle finger and the forefinger of the left hand. The total number of sticks held between the fingers of the left hand will be 9 or 5. In the first round the single stick between the little finger and the ring finger is discounted, making the total number 8 or 4. The number 8 is given the value 2 and the number 4 is given the value 3. The resulting value is written down and used to determine the value of the line together with the results of round 2 and round 3. After the value has been determined the sticks between the fingers of the left hand are set aside for the duration of the remaining two rounds.

Round 2:

Gather up all the sticks left on the table into one big bundle and split it randomly into two bundles. Repeat the complete procedure described for round 1. When the sticks of both bundles have been counted off, the total number of sticks between the fingers of the left hand will be 8 or 4, including the single stick picked from the right hand bundle at the beginning of this round. Again the number 8 is given the value 2 and the number 4 the value 3. This value is written down and the sticks between the fingers of the left hand are set aside for the duration of the third and last round.

Round 3:

The sticks now remaining on the table are gathered up again into one bundle. This bundle is randomly split into two bundles and the procedure described for round 1 is repeated for the third time. Also this time the total number of sticks between the fingers of the left hand will be 8 (value 2) or 4 (value 3), including the single stick between the little finger and the ring finger. Again the resulting value is written down.

The resulting values of the first, second, and third rounds are added up to determine the value of the line. In our *top down method* the first three rounds determine the value of the *top line*. This value will be 9 for a moving Yang line (a solid line with a circle in the middle), 8 for a static Yin line (a broken line), 7 for a static Yang line (a solid line), or 6 for a moving Yin line (a broken line with a cross in the middle).

The same method as described above is used when the reader chooses to assemble the hexagram *from the bottom up*. In that case the first three rounds will determine the value of the *bottom line*.

To obtain the next line down all 49 sticks are gathered up again into one big bundle to repeat the whole procedure of three rounds described above. This procedure is repeated in total six times to obtain all six lines of the hexagram which represents the oracle's answer to the reader's question.

Example (using top down method)
Result in numbers, obtained after manipulating the sticks:

- 1st three rounds: 9(2)+8(2)+4(3)=7
- 2nd three rounds: 5(3)+4(3)+8(2)=8
- 3rd three rounds: 5(3)+4(3)+4(3)=9
- 4th three rounds: 9(2)+4(3)+4(3)=8
- 5th three rounds: 9(2)+8(2)+8(2)=6
- 6th three rounds: 5(3)+8(2)+8(2)=7

The following diagram shows the translation of the numbers into a line diagram (hexagram) and how this hexagram changes into a different hexagram as a result of the moving lines changing into their opposites (Yang becomes Yin and Yin becomes Yang; see for more detail chapter 3 of this book).

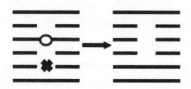

Hexagram 21 with moving lines changes into hexagram 41.

2.4.2 The coin method

This method for consulting the oracle uses three identical coins. Just like dice the coins need to be uniform, i.e. three coins of the same denomination and the same currency. These coins should be used only for consulting the oracle. It is important that they are new and clean and, preferably, have not been in circulation.

Toss the coins in one hand and roll them like dice on a hard, flat, clutter-free surface. For the interpretation of the result the value 3 is assigned to a head and the value 2 to a tail. The sum of the values of the coins as they have fallen is the value of the line.

There are four possible combinations:

- Three heads   3+3+3=9 (moving Yang) or
- Two heads + one tail   3+3+2=8 (static Yin) or
- One head + two tails   3+2+2=7 (static Yang) or
- Three tails   2+2+2=6 (moving Yin)

In our *top down method* the first toss of the coins gives the top line. After the first toss the coins are tossed five more times to obtain the remaining lines of the hexagram.

Example (using top down method)

Result in numbers, obtained after throwing the coins:

- 1st toss: three heads   3+3+3=9
- 2nd toss: two heads + one tail   3+3+2=8
- 3rd toss: one head + two tails   3+2+2=7
- 4th toss: three tails   2+2+2=6
- 5th toss: two heads + one tail   3+3+2=8
- 6th toss: one head + two tails   3+2+2=7

The following diagram shows the translation of the numbers into a line diagram (hexagram) and how this hexagram changes into a different hexagram as a result of the moving lines changing into their opposites (Yang becomes Yin and Yin becomes Yang; see for more detail chapter 3 of this book).

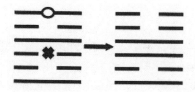

Hexagram 21 with moving lines changes into hexagram 55.

Chapter 3

Interpreting the result of an I Ching consultation

3.1 General principles

When consulting the oracle, using either sticks or coins, the reader will construct a diagram as shown in the examples in the previous section. The resulting diagram will show one of these three possibilities:

- a hexagram with a single moving line
- a hexagram with multiple moving lines
- a hexagram without moving lines, i.e. a static hexagram

If the reader receives in an I Ching consultation a hexagram with one or more moving lines, the moving lines will transform the initial hexagram into a different hexagram (the outcome hexagram) according to the following rule.

When a Yang line moves, it changes into a Yin line.

When a Yin line moves, it changes into a Yang line.

Using the **Key for Identifying the Hexagrams** the reader will be able to identify the number of the hexagram corresponding with the diagram the reader constructed during the consultation. In Part II of this book the reader will find the interpretive texts for the 64 hexagrams and their individual lines.

The individual lines in a hexagram are numbered from the bottom to the top, starting with line 1 at the bottom and ending with line 6 at the top (see diagram below).

Hexagram 59
Dispersion

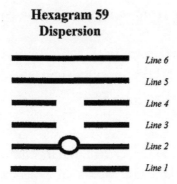

If the reader receives a hexagram with a single moving line, the texts of the initial hexagram, the moving line in this hexagram, and the outcome hexagram will apply (see our examples in chapter **3.2.1 A hexagram with a single moving line**).

The interpretation of multiple moving lines is more complex (see our explanation and examples in chapter **3.2.2 A hexagram with multiple moving lines**).

If the reader receives a static hexagram, only the texts of this hexagram and its inner hexagram will apply (see our examples in chapter **3.2.3 Static hexagrams and inner hexagrams**).

To help the reader understand how the I Ching presents information in the form of hexagrams and moving lines, we have selected some examples from our own I Ching consultations. These examples describe actual events in our own life, captured and chronicled by the I Ching in hexagrams and moving lines. We have also included a *time factor* in every example, giving an idea of the time periods involved in these experiences. The events represented by the hexagrams and the moving lines can take weeks, months, or longer to unfold. There is no fixed rule for this. Some hexagrams represent experiences covering a long period of time, sometimes several years. A hexagram with a single moving line can occasionally portray a fast-moving experience.

3.2 Examples from our own I Ching consultations

3.2.1 A hexagram with a single moving line

A moving line describes a specific experience, decision, or event, which will bring about a change in the reader's situation. A single moving line changes the initial hexagram into a different hexagram, the outcome hexagram. The outcome hexagram is the result of whatever is occurring in the moving line.

To illustrate how this works in practice, here are three examples from our own I Ching consultations.

Example 1

We were in a situation in which we had invested a lot of hope and energy, but unfortunately, it was fast becoming a disappointing and discouraging experience. Nevertheless, it was very difficult for us to let go and admit defeat, especially because we had worked very hard trying to make a success of it.

We asked the I Ching if we should give up on the situation and leave. We received a single moving line in hexagram *Dispersion*.

Hexagram 59
Dispersion

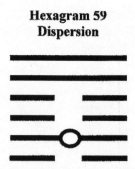

Dispersion represents a time when egoistic ideas or rigid attitudes break up, opening the way for real progress. The Experiencer is forced to abandon a cherished plan, because it is not going to succeed. This is a painful experience which cannot be avoided.

The second line of *Dispersion* told us to stop trying to make a success of a hopeless situation. It advised us to leave and retreat to a safe haven, which in our case meant going home. We left a few days later.

The second line transforms hexagram *Dispersion* into hexagram *The View*.

The View is a vantage point and a safe haven where the

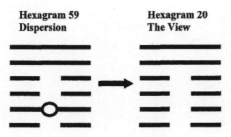

Hexagram 59
Dispersion

Hexagram 20
The View

Experiencer can review his/her life. *The View* also represents a crossroads in life; it is a time when choices can be made and a new initiative can be undertaken.

After returning home we spent time making a review of our life together, our past successes and failures, and the implications of these experiences for the future. We decided to resume work on an important project we had earlier abandoned.

The time period covered by *The View* lasted for nearly a year, culminating in the completion of our project.

Example 2

Several years ago we consulted the I Ching when we were considering making an application for an interesting job. We received a single moving line in hexagram *The Well*.

Hexagram 48
The Well

The Well represents the communal well, which is the source of societal nourishment everybody needs to draw from. This nourishment can take the form of job opportunities, housing or any other area in which one needs to make societal progress.

The third line of *The Well* told us we would not succeed in getting the job; our experience would not be recognized, even though we were highly suitable for the work.

Nevertheless, we applied for the job anyway and, not surprisingly, were rejected.

The third line transforms hexagram *The Well* into hexagram *The Power of Flowing Water*.

Hexagram 48
The Well

Hexagram 29
The Power of
Flowing Water

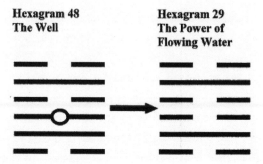

The Power of Flowing Water represents the power to be strong and persevering while pushing one's way through difficult circumstances. In this situation the way to success is through sincerity and integrity. It is essential to find the right way to act and then move forward with the strength of true intent; this is the only way to make any progress.

The job rejection prompted us to follow a new direction in life and we galvanized into action with a new plan. With a strong sense of purpose we pushed our way through a series of very problematic situations and eventually succeeded in winning through. The whole experience unfolded over a period of three months.

Example 3

We were living in a beautiful place in which we had experienced a lot of happiness and peace. However, we were not making any societal progress; work was hard to find, and because we were outsiders, we came up against a good deal of mistrust.

We decided to ask the I Ching if we should move to a different country and make a new start. We received a single moving line in hexagram *Peace*.

Peace can represent a very fruitful period of fulfilling activity or

Hexagram 11
Peace

a time of great happiness and peace after a period of struggle and misfortune. However, sooner or later the time of *Peace* will begin to wane, because *Peace* cannot be maintained indefinitely.

The second line of *Peace* told us we would be unable to make any further progress in our current location. It advised us to look towards the future and find a way to travel to a new destination.

The second line transforms hexagram *Peace* into hexagram *The Darkening of the Light*.

Hexagram 11   **Hexagram 36**
Peace   **The darkening**
                                    of the light

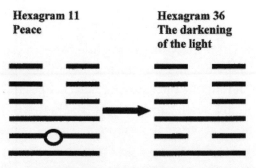

The Darkening of the Light represents dark times when wicked or mediocre people have the upper hand, blocking and marginalizing those who truly want to work for progress and the common good. It is also a time when the future is obscured and the challenge is to find a way through the darkness.

After a long journey we arrived at a new location to make a new beginning and entered the scenario described in hexagram *The Darkening of the Light*. The change of location gave us security and a nice home, but some very unpleasant people were dominating the situation. The difficulties we experienced at our new location nearly overwhelmed us and for a long time we were unable to see far enough ahead to make any plans for the future.

The entire experience lasted for over a year. We eventually had to abandon the situation and move on.

The second line of hexagram *Peace* is a good example of moving lines in hexagrams which seem to contradict the experience the hexagram itself represents. This line is actually leaving the experience of *Peace*, because the time of *Peace* has come to an end.

3.2.2 A hexagram with multiple moving lines

If the reader receives a hexagram with two or more moving lines in an I Ching consultation, a whole sequence of hexagrams will unfold. It is only possible to receive *one moving line in a single hexagram*; any subsequent moving lines appear one by one in an unfolding sequence of hexagrams. Multiple moving lines are like a series of steps, climbing up from one hexagram to the next. The sequence of events represented by multiple moving lines always begins at the lowest moving line of the initial hexagram. The lowest moving line transforms the initial hexagram into another hexagram; the next moving line changes that hexagram into another and so on until the last (the highest) moving line produces the final outcome hexagram. The outcome hexagram represents the culmination of the entire experience.

Multiple moving lines represent different stages of a longer term development as they move upward through the sequence of hexagrams. Each moving line describes an event or a process of change which will occur over a certain time period.

Although multiple moving lines often represent lengthy time periods, they can occasionally portray an experience that covers a very brief time span, possibly a few days or weeks. In such a case the series of hexagrams and moving lines blurs into a single continuous experience without interludes or "dead periods".

To illustrate how a hexagram with multiple moving lines unfolds into a whole sequence of hexagrams, here are two examples from our own I Ching consultations.

Example 1

We were living and working at a location in a foreign land. The work was intensive and very demanding; it was also stimulating and completely absorbing. Everything went perfectly well until the management decided to renege on a promise they had previously made to us. We were very unhappy with this decision and wondered if it would be better for us to leave.

We decided to ask the I Ching if we should continue to work for these people. We received hexagram *Treading Correctly* with a series of four moving lines, as shown in the following diagram.

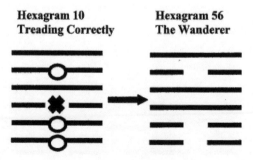

Hexagram 10
Treading Correctly

Hexagram 56
The Wanderer

This series unfolds into a sequence of four hexagrams, each with a single moving line, ending with *The Wanderer* as the final outcome hexagram.

The first moving line in this series is the first line of hexagram *Treading Correctly*.

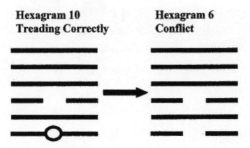

Hexagram 10
Treading Correctly

Hexagram 6
Conflict

Treading Correctly heralds a time of transition; it means anticipating developments and taking strong action when the time is ripe. Coping with unreasonable people is a challenging aspect of this experience.

The people we depended on to give us a fair deal in the workplace were proving to be stubborn and unreasonable. They seemed to have no problems breaking their promises and assumed we would accept any decisions they chose to make.

The first line of *Treading Correctly* advised us to give up on any ambitions in our current situation and follow an independent path. We were on our own and should act accordingly.

The first line transforms hexagram *Treading Correctly* into hexagram *Conflict*.

The next moving line in this series is the second line of hexagram *Conflict*.

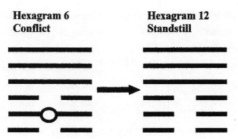

Hexagram 6
Conflict

Hexagram 12
Standstill

Conflict represents a situation in which there is a great risk of becoming involved in a serious conflict, an unpleasant and time-consuming struggle which should be avoided at all costs.

The second line of *Conflict* advised us to disengage and prepare to leave the situation to avoid the risk of being drawn into a nasty conflict.

We realized that further discussions would be fruitless and the time had come to make a plan to move on. The management had no intention of keeping to their promises, but any confrontation with them would only lead to a conflict in which we would be the losers.

The second line transforms hexagram *Conflict* into hexagram *Standstill*.

The third moving line in this series is the third line of hexagram *Standstill*.

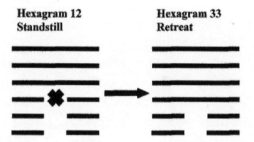

**Hexagram 12
Standstill**

**Hexagram 33
Retreat**

Standstill represents a time of stagnation when real progress is no longer possible, because the wrong people are in power.

The third line of *Standstill* told us the people in power would feel ashamed when confronted with the result of their own selfishness.

Several days later we told the management of our intention to leave. It was obvious why we were leaving; they had not kept to their side of the bargain. We could see they were ashamed, but they were too stubborn to change their minds.

The third line transforms hexagram *Standstill* into hexagram *Retreat*.

The last moving line of this series is the fifth line of hexagram *Retreat*.

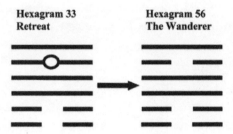

Hexagram 33
Retreat

Hexagram 56
The Wanderer

Retreat represents the necessity to withdraw from a situation in which mediocre people have the upper hand. Their unreasonable attitudes and lack of willingness to cooperate make any attempt to establish a positive dialogue impossible.

The fifth line of *Retreat* told us we would be able to make a smooth exit from the situation, without any unpleasantness or difficulty.

We made a travel plan and set a date for our departure. Everything went perfectly.

The fifth line transforms hexagram *Retreat* into the final outcome hexagram, *The Wanderer*. This hexagram represents a long journey, a major transition from one location to another.

We left the place where we had been living and working for nearly a year and made the long journey back home.

This entire experience, which began with hexagram *Treading* and ended with hexagram *The Wanderer*, lasted for only one month.

Example 2

We were looking for job opportunities, but it was proving difficult to find an opening anywhere. An economic slowdown with rising unemployment was fast creating a situation in which opportunities were becoming hard to find.

We asked the I Ching if we should continue our search for an opportunity at this time. We received hexagram *Modesty* with a series of three moving lines, as represented in the following diagram.

Hexagram 15
Modesty

Hexagram 4
Caution and
Restraint

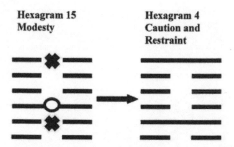

This series unfolds into a sequence of three hexagrams, each with a single moving line, ending with *Caution and Restraint* as the final outcome hexagram.

The first moving line in this series is the second line of hexagram *Modesty*.

Hexagram15
Modesty

Hexagram 46
Authentic
Development

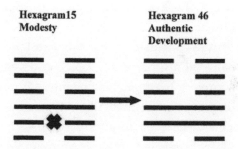

Modesty is about accepting the reality as it is, even though things have turned out to be far from perfect. The time has come to take responsibility for the choices one has made and look for realistic ways to make progress.

The second line of *Modesty* told us to continue with our efforts, because we would eventually succeed in finding real opportunities.

We continued our job search, focusing on areas in which we had a lot of experience to offer.

The second line transforms hexagram *Modesty* into hexagram *Authentic Development*.

The next moving line in this series is the third line of hexagram *Authentic Development*.

Hexagram 46
Authentic
Development

Hexagram 7

The Army

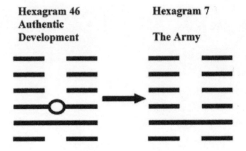

Authentic Development means following a higher aim in life through exploring and developing one's hidden talents. This is a period of personal growth which will eventually lead to finding new opportunities.

The third line of *Authentic Development* advised us to engage in a systematic search for opportunities in order to find out what is truly feasible.

We came to the conclusion we needed to look for work in an area we had real affinity with. Many years earlier we had worked on a project for homeless people which had been a very rewarding experience. We liked the idea of returning to social work and decided to give it a try. Over a period of several months we contacted various groups and organizations, most of which were not interested in us. Some were not hiring; others only hired people who could show recent experience. Nevertheless, we eventually succeeded in attracting the interest of a big organization which was running a number of social projects. They invited us to make an application; this involved a lot of paperwork which turned out to be very time-consuming.

We pressed ahead with the job application anyway, determined to make a breakthrough. During this process we saw the workings of a very extensive and complicated bureaucracy, a bloated organization with several layers of administrative functions. We soon arrived at a point where we needed to ask a number of questions about the financial details of the work contract. We approached them by telephone and e-mail. Our e-mails often went unanswered and telephone calls yielded little or nothing. No matter how hard we tried, it was impossible to get any detailed information out of them. Every person we contacted turned out to be unhelpful or vague.

The third line transforms hexagram *Authentic Development* into hexagram *The Army*.

The last moving line in this series is the sixth line of hexagram *The Army*.

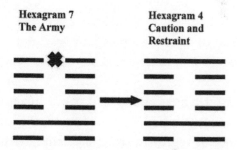

Hexagram 7
The Army

Hexagram 4
Caution and Restraint

The Army represents a time when it is essential to forge ahead and overcome difficulties by adopting an effective strategy and following it through to the end.

The sixth line of *The Army* told us we would be able to make a breakthrough, but only after severing relations with untrustworthy people.

We decided to give up on this job application and approach a completely different organization. This time it worked; we applied for a job and within a month we were accepted.

However, the sixth line of *The Army* also told us we would have to work hard to consolidate our success.

The organization had accepted us for the job and we were very determined to make a success of this opportunity.

The sixth line transforms hexagram *The Army* into the final outcome hexagram, *Caution and Restraint*. This hexagram represents a situation in which things are not what they appear to be. People are capable of cleverly misrepresenting themselves and therefore it is important to be very cautious.

We were entering unknown territory and would have to move very carefully. This entire experience, ending in the hexagram *Caution and Restraint,* covered a period of seven months.

The ending is obviously inconclusive; we had succeeded in finding a job, but the future was still unclear. The I Ching had given us an accurate description of our search for an opportunity, culminating in the sixth line of *The Army* which told us we would succeed. However, this success would eventually lead to the ambiguous situation described in hexagram *Caution and Restraint.* At that point we would need to go back to the I Ching for more guidance. This illustrates how essential it is to consult the oracle regularly in times of uncertainty or confusion.

3.2.3 Static hexagrams and inner hexagrams

A *static hexagram* is a hexagram without moving lines.

Static hexagrams represent situations that have a momentum of their own and will inevitably change. This process of change is predictable, often occurring slowly over a long period of time. The reader may be locked in a time period in which nothing seems to change, but change is nevertheless slowly gathering pace. He/she will need to follow a strategy based on a clear insight into the current situation and the nature of the change that is gathering momentum.

A *static hexagram* describes the reader's present situation and advises the reader how to respond in an intelligent and effective way. It contains an *inner hexagram* which represents the process of change that is going to transform the situation. When the reader studies the *inner hexagram* he/she will be able to see the nature of the change that is, or will be, driving events.

The reader should only read the texts of the *static hexagram* and its *inner hexagram;* the texts of the lines of the hexagrams do not apply. In the **Table of Hexagrams and Inner Hexagrams** (appendix at the end of this book) the reader can find the *inner hexagram* of every hexagram.

The following two examples illustrate how to interpret a *static hexagram* and how the *inner hexagram* is actually determined.

Example 1

We wanted to rent a house, but we had to convince the owners that we would be reliable tenants. This meant having to go through a thorough vetting procedure which involved a lot of paperwork and getting several references. We wondered if this effort was going to be worthwhile and decided to consult the I Ching.

We received hexagram 61 *Trust* as a *static hexagram*.

Hexagram 61
Trust

Hexagram *Trust* told us we would succeed in convincing the owners of our honesty and good intentions, but this would take considerable effort.

We engaged in the vetting procedure, produced the required references and eventually succeeded in obtaining the tenancy. After a lot of effort we had managed to convince the owners we would be reliable and trustworthy tenants.

The *inner hexagram* of hexagram 61 *Trust* is hexagram 27 *Seeking Nourishment*.

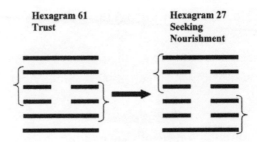

The parentheses in the diagram show how the inner trigrams of the *static hexagram* 61 become the upper and lower primary trigrams of the *inner hexagram* 27.

Seeking Nourishment represents a major effort to find societal nourishment. It is necessary to be very discerning in order to find the right people and the specific area that can provide nourishment. This is the only way the search for nourishment can succeed.

Getting the tenancy gave us the nourishment we needed. The house was in a great location and we could focus on developing our interests and activities. The entire process took nearly three months.

Example 2

We were planning to contact an organization we had previously worked for to see if they had any work available. However, we felt unsure about it and wondered if it would be the right thing to do. We decided to ask the I Ching if we should move forward with this plan.

We received hexagram 25 *Following the Will of Heaven* as a *static hexagram*.

Hexagram 25
Following the
Will of Heaven

Hexagram *Following the Will of Heaven* urged us not to carry out any plans at that time. There was a real risk of acting prematurely or making disastrous decisions. We were told to step back and let events unfold in their own way. Over time it would become clear what we were really meant to do.

This advice confirmed our own doubts and uncertainties. Our plan was obviously not going to lead anywhere. We had to hold on and keep our minds open for other solutions. In the meantime our circumstances became more and more difficult until our situation reached a complete standstill. We realized we would have to make a major transition to a new location, where we could make a new start, but we did not yet know how.

The *inner hexagram* of hexagram 25 *Following the Will of Heaven* is hexagram 53 *Working towards a Goal*.

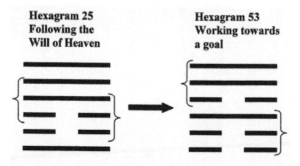

The parentheses in the diagram show how the inner trigrams of the *static hexagram* 25 become the upper and lower primary trigrams of the *inner hexagram* 53.

Working towards a Goal represents the slow process of developing a realistic aim and working step by step towards achieving it.

We had considerable difficulty finding a way to make the transition to a new location. We researched several options, many of which proved to be unrealistic or impossible to achieve. Eventually we managed to identify a good location that was affordable and completely realistic. Step by step we worked towards making the transition to this location.

The entire effort lasted for nearly a year, but we succeeded in the end, and moved to a place where we could make a new start.

Part II

The 64 Hexagrams

1

The Creative

In this hexagram the I Ching uses the image of Heaven, a timeless place of radiant light which is the source of all creative power.

The Creative symbolizes the light which even in the darkest of situations cannot be completely extinguished. The creative force, which will prevail against all the odds, is the power of goodness and truthfulness. By following a path of truth and sincerity the Experiencer will emerge unscathed from the changes and challenges that lie ahead.

The power to follow a way through impossible circumstances and nevertheless find solutions has an almost magical quality in the time of *The Creative*. The Experiencer's great inner strength provides the power to endure and succeed, no matter how long it takes. He/she will need to draw from this reservoir of power during a challenging period of constant difficulties, including coping with problematic or downright hostile people.

The Experiencer has the vigor and the staying power to persevere in an important undertaking and see it through. He/she has the capacity to maintain a high level of creative energy regardless of setbacks. Indeed, time is on the side of the Experiencer; he/she will win through in the end.

The moving lines

Line 1

The time to act has not yet come. Any attempts to make a breakthrough now would be premature, because there are no genuine opportunities at this time. The Experiencer is advised to continue in the present circumstances until he/she has gained a clearer understanding of the situation.

Line 2

The Experiencer is looking for opportunities to link up with others and engage in meaningful work. He/she has great personal qualities and considerable potential, but lacks connections and useful contacts. The Experiencer will need to stay true to his/her ideals and continue to follow an independent path.

Line 3

The Experiencer is making a major effort to try to improve an extremely difficult situation. He/she is facing serious opposition and there is an increasing risk of losing support and becoming isolated. This is an anxiety-provoking experience. The Experiencer will need to be cautious and very diplomatic in his/her dealings with the other players in the situation. In this way the Experiencer will avoid making any serious mistakes.

Line 4

The Experiencer is actively searching for ways to make progress, but is uncertain and cannot as yet see the way forward. The times are unfavorable and it will be difficult to get recognition or find genuine opportunities during this period. It is absolutely crucial to follow the way of the heart and stay true to one's fundamental beliefs.

Line 5

The Experiencer is in a position to make significant progress. His/her personal qualities will be recognized and opportunities will open up. The Experiencer has the resources to engage in a major undertaking and succeed.

Line 6

The Experiencer is becoming increasingly isolated and is in danger of losing touch with the reality. He/she is wasting time and energy on an overambitious attempt to score a success. To continue in this way would lead to exhaustion and failure. The Experiencer is advised to give up on his/her ambitions; otherwise there will be cause for regret.

2

The Receptive

In this hexagram the I Ching uses the image of the Earth, the arena in which the human drama is played over and over again.

The Receptive represents the entire field of activity – the economic and social dynamic of organized hierarchical society. *The Receptive* also represents the receptive mind, experiencing and responding to events. In this context the Experiencer is a receptacle, open and receptive to powerful societal imperatives. Therefore the necessity to socially engage and cooperate with others in order to achieve any success is an essential aspect of this hexagram.

The Experiencer is looking for a way to engage in the field of activity, particularly in something that can provide a fulfilling experience or an important breakthrough.

To have any chance of achieving a lasting success the Experiencer will have to find a true purpose in life and focus on a concrete goal, otherwise he/she will just be blown by the wind. It is crucial to maintain one's independence of spirit, because the Experiencer cannot afford to throw him/herself away and become subservient to mediocre people.

The Experiencer should resist trying to force any progress; otherwise he/she will risk going off on a tangent and lose the way. It will not be possible to speed things up, because events must be allowed to unfold at their own pace. By following developments and keeping an open mind the Experiencer will be in a position to see potential opportunities as they arise.

Considerable perseverance is needed during this time, regardless of disappointments, which cannot be avoided. The Experiencer must continue to believe in his/her ability to succeed. Success will come in the end, but it may take a long time coming.

The moving lines

Line 1

The Experiencer's current circumstances will not be sustainable over the longer term. The situation will gradually deteriorate and eventually fall into serious decline. It will not be possible to prevent this. The Experiencer can already see the first signs of deterioration and cannot afford to be complacent. The time has come to withdraw from the situation and seriously consider a way to make a transition.

Line 2

The Experiencer should not try to contrive anything. He/she just needs to be open-minded and follow the guidance of events. Over time everything will naturally fall into place of its own accord.

Line 3

This is a time of limitations. The Experiencer has talent and expertise, but has to play a subordinate role. In this situation the Experiencer is not receiving the full recognition he/she deserves. Nevertheless, the Experiencer has the strength of character to continue his/her work with modesty and magnanimity. In this way it will be possible to accomplish an important task.

Line 4

Great caution is advised. The Experiencer has awoken the darkness in others. He/she is at risk of becoming the target of people's mad jealousies and destructive tendencies. The Experiencer is advised to withdraw and quietly carry on with his/her daily activities, allowing events to unfold at their own pace. Over time a new perspective will open up in the situation and it will become possible to take action.

Line 5

The Experiencer is called upon to serve in an important, but subservient position. By acting in a discreet and diplomatic way the Experiencer can have a beneficial influence on the situation.

Line 6

The darkness in others will now have to be openly resisted. The Experiencer's presence in the current situation has drawn out the unpleasant tendencies of wicked people. The situation will reach a climax in a fateful struggle between the Experiencer and his/ her opponents. Both sides will be damaged, but the Experiencer will not be defeated. Nevertheless, for the Experiencer this will mark the beginning of the end of his/her involvement in the situation.

3

Difficulty in Making a Beginning
In this hexagram the I Ching uses the image of a thunderstorm to illustrate confusion and chaos.

The Experiencer is confused and cannot see how to overcome the present difficulties. His/her way of life is slowly coming to an end and nothing is yet materializing to replace it. A search for opportunities has proven to be painstakingly slow, often yielding little or no result. Attempts to link up with others in an effort to make a breakthrough have thus far only led the Experiencer into ambiguous and confusing situations that have been stressful and frustrating.

Difficulty in Making a Beginning is often caused by the Experiencer's desire to prolong an old lifestyle that no longer has any relevance in the reality. He/she is clinging to an old way of thinking while spending a lot of time on a wasted effort to continue with a way of life that belongs to the past. The tremendous challenge facing the Experiencer is to create a viable and durable new way of life; otherwise the same disappointing experiences will keep recurring.

The Experiencer has the strength of character to make a realistic assessment of his/her situation. The first step will be to thoroughly examine any possible opportunities and try to separate the chaff from the wheat. However, a lot of patience and optimism will be needed to find a way to make a new beginning. The Experiencer is advised to seek help and support from others during this difficult period. A new beginning will eventually materialize and the Experiencer will be able to start a new life.

The moving lines

Line 1
Confronted with unforeseen obstacles the Experiencer hesitates and wonders whether to move forward with his/her plan. This is not the right opportunity for making a new beginning. The Experiencer is advised to hold back and seek advice.

Line 2
The Experiencer is facing increasing difficulties and progress has ground to a halt. His/her plans for making a new beginning are sound, but this is not the right time to move forward. The Experiencer is advised to be patient and live within the current limitations until a way through opens up.

Line 3
The Experiencer's plan is ill-conceived and based on insufficient knowledge of the situation. Continuing in this way would lead to a humiliating failure. The Experiencer is strongly advised to concentrate on reaching a better understanding of the current situation and refrain from taking any new initiatives during this time.

Line 4
The Experiencer has been making a major effort to make a new start in very challenging circumstances. However, the situation

is proving to be impossible and the Experiencer is faced with the difficulty of having to let go and admit defeat. He/she will have to stop being indecisive and come to terms with the reality. The Experiencer is strongly advised to leave the situation and follow an independent path. Making a transition will lead to a new beginning in happier circumstances.

Line 5
The Experiencer is trying to link up with others in an attempt to make a new start. Unfortunately his/her good intentions are meeting with distrust and misunderstanding. The Experiencer should not continue trying to make progress in this way. The time has come to withdraw and focus on finding a completely different direction in life.

Line 6
A deeply painful experience has led to a situation in which the Experiencer is completely marginalized. This cannot be allowed to continue any longer. The Experiencer is strongly advised to break free and leave this unfortunate episode behind.

4

Caution and Restraint

In this hexagram the I Ching uses the imagery of a mountain with a deep abyss in front of it. A figure is standing on the edge of the abyss, looking at the mountain, perplexed and wondering how to proceed.

The Experiencer has arrived at an impasse and cannot see how to proceed. Confused and anxious, the Experiencer is completely in the dark, in a situation that is riddled with difficulties. Unaware of the pitfalls that lie ahead, the Experiencer is in risky territory and will have to be very alert and keep an open mind. Therefore it is crucial not to act on impulse, but to hold back and take the time to study the situation. With patience and caution the Experiencer will gradually understand what his/her position is in the framework of things.

There is something very deceptive about this situation; things are not what they appear to be. It is extremely important to be very realistic, because any illusions about the situation will reduce the Experiencer's ability to act effectively; a mistaken action could lead to disastrous consequences. The Experiencer is in a weak position and cannot afford to have any misconceptions or grand ideas, which could easily backfire.

During this period the Experiencer will have to learn to deal with selfish people who are capable of cleverly misrepresenting themselves. If the Experiencer is in a position of dependency, it will be very important to maintain personal dignity and independence of spirit. No matter how strong the desire may be to make progress, nothing will be achieved by conforming to the unreasonable expectations and demands of others. The only way forward is to develop a clear purpose and be very resolute in following a longer term aim. This may involve discarding people and situations that have proven to be worthless.

The moving lines

Line 1
The Experiencer cannot continue in this way. It is time to get serious and really think about things. The Experiencer will have to develop clearer aims and a real sense of purpose; otherwise things will start to go downhill.

Line 2
During this period the Experiencer will need to be diplomatic and try to accept the weaknesses and flaws of others, even when they are failing to live up to their responsibilities. The Experiencer is not in a very strong position, but can have a positive influence on the situation by being considerate and good mannered. In this way the Experiencer can maintain his/her somewhat precarious position.

Line 3
The Experiencer is at risk of becoming mesmerized by attractive people, who are actually unreliable and cannot be trusted. The Experiencer has lost his/her sense of direction in life and will need to focus on the task of developing a new purpose.

Line 4

The Experiencer has lost touch with the reality and is making unrealistic plans which will lead nowhere. A major effort will have to be made to come to grips with the present reality. The Experiencer will need to work towards finding realistic solutions, with the aim of eventually making a transition.

Line 5

The Experiencer is open-minded and prepared to learn. These qualities are invaluable and will enable the Experiencer to grow spiritually through personal development. As a result the Experiencer will be able to find the right way forward and follow the path of destiny.

Line 6

It is time to take strong action against arrogant and misguided people. In doing so the Experiencer should take care to conduct him/herself in a correct and disciplined manner.

Waiting for Nourishment
In this hexagram the I Ching uses the imagery of dense clouds moving across the sky, bringing the promise of rain. When the rain comes, everything will be nourished.

Pleasant surroundings and a comfortable lifestyle are becoming overshadowed by a deep concern for the future. There is an uneasy feeling that time is running out. With growing anxiety the Experiencer is wondering if the current situation will be sustainable over the longer term.

When the Experiencer is ready to see the situation as it really is and realize just how precarious his/her position has become, a plan to get out will slowly emerge. This plan may seem very ambitious and almost impossible to accomplish, but the Experiencer is challenged to believe in his/her ability to succeed and carry out the plan with confidence and optimism.

Once a decision is reached, it is crucial to act without hesitation. There is a limited window of opportunity. Furthermore, there is a real risk of being overtaken by events and becoming entangled in serious difficulties. The Experiencer has the energy and vision to set a plan in motion that will create the conditions for a major transition. It is essential to be resolute and follow this plan right through to the end.

There will be a period of waiting for results, which may be stressful, but the Experiencer can calmly and confidently await a positive outcome. In *Waiting for Nourishment* events will gather a momentum of their own and then everything will come together.

The moving lines

Line 1
There is no future in the present situation and a transition to another location will eventually become urgent. However, the Experiencer can afford to carefully plan the next move and avoid making a hasty and badly-conceived plan of departure.

Line 2
The situation is deteriorating and there is some friction with other people. The Experiencer will be subject to criticism or malicious gossip. He/she is in a strong position and will not need to be too concerned about this. The Experiencer can afford to wait for the situation to unfold until an opportunity presents itself to get out of the present difficulties.

Line 3
The Experiencer has acted prematurely and this is going to result in repercussions. He/she will have to tread very carefully and, if necessary, be prepared to defend his/her interests. In this way the Experiencer will be able to hold his/her ground and remain free from damage.

Line 4
The Experiencer has been overtaken by events and is now in acute danger. He/she should not wait any longer, but take resolute action to get out of this predicament.

Line 5

The Experiencer is advised to enjoy this time and take a rest from the difficult journey through life. It is also an ideal opportunity to reflect and make plans for the future.

Line 6

The Experiencer is getting into serious difficulties which cannot be avoided. There is nothing he/she can do about it. Events will take an unexpected turn and lead to a surprising encounter with strangers. The Experiencer will need to maintain an open and flexible attitude and be very diplomatic. Eventually, everything will work out for the best.

6

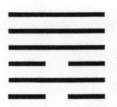

Conflict

The hexagram *Conflict* represents a situation in which there is a great danger of pursuing an ambitious aim that would lead the Experiencer into a serious conflict. Engaging in a conflict at this time with the idea of winning could have disastrous consequences. The Experiencer is strongly advised to turn away from the world of petty people with selfish interests and follow a higher path.

The Experiencer will need to proceed carefully in order to avoid an all-out conflict. He/she is not in a position of power or influence and cannot afford to be drawn into a serious dispute. No matter how strong the desire may be to make progress, the Experiencer will have to come to terms with the limited options available in this situation. It is crucial to avoid taking any hasty initiatives, which would only lead to a damaging conflict with powerful established interests. Before embarking upon any action the Experiencer will need to determine what the possible consequences might be. It may be necessary to ask for professional advice.

In the meantime the Experiencer can withdraw into his/her circle of friends and avoid conflict by finding a way to circumvent the current difficulties.

The moving lines

Line 1

This is a time to be diplomatic and avoid being drawn into quarrels and disagreements. The aim is to find a way through a difficult situation by creating as little friction as possible. Everything will be resolved in the end.

Line 2

To avoid a serious conflict the Experiencer is advised to withdraw and disengage as much as possible. There is no blame in this; it is simply not possible to achieve anything in these circumstances. The Experiencer should be prepared to leave the situation and move on when the opportunity arises.

Line 3

The Experiencer should resist any tempting offers or proposals during this time, because these would lead to serious difficulties or conflict. The Experiencer is advised to be content with his/her present position and not try to get recognition or promotion.

Line 4

The Experiencer is advised to let go of a conflict which cannot be won. He/she will need to step back and find a different way to deal with the situation. This will make it possible to resolve the conflict.

Line 5

The Experiencer will be able to win a conflict against an unreasonable opponent by involving an independent arbiter who will uphold the Experiencer's case. In this way a potentially nasty dispute will be brought to an end and enable the Experiencer to make a fresh start.

Line 6

The Experiencer has fought a conflict until the bitter end. He/she has won, but it is a Pyrrhic victory. The conflict has not really been resolved; it is still simmering and the Experiencer will eventually become exhausted.

The Army

This hexagram represents two possible scenarios.

The first scenario is a situation in which the Experiencer is called upon to give leadership to people in difficult circumstances. His/her sincerity and desire to work for the common good will succeed in drawing people together to take action and overcome problems.

The second scenario shows the Experiencer coming to grips with outstanding problems in his/her own life and decisively putting an end to recurring difficulties.

The Army heralds a time to forge ahead and overcome difficulties by adopting a strategy and following it through to the end. When the Experiencer has properly identified the outstanding problems preventing further progress, he/she can devise an effective plan to successfully overcome the obstacles. The Experiencer will need the qualities of self-leadership, discipline and self-control to galvanize his/her resources and take the necessary action. Iron determination is essential to be able to press forward and succeed. The Experiencer will have to be prepared to take risks whenever necessary and, above all else, believe in his/her power to break through and win.

The moving lines

Line 1
The Experiencer is energized and optimistic and wants to press ahead, but any impulsive moves now will lead to disaster. The Experiencer will need to take the time to devise a sensible and coherent plan of action in order to achieve success.

Line 2
The Experiencer is reaching the point where he/she will be able to make a decisive breakthrough. This will lead to success and recognition.

Line 3
The Experiencer is being thwarted in his/her efforts to achieve a solution in a problematic situation. A lack of collective leadership and proper coordination has led to a defeat or a serious setback. The Experiencer will have to completely rethink his/her strategy and develop a new plan of action.

Line 4
The Experiencer is trying to achieve something against impossible odds. He/she will have to give up on this plan and move on. As a result the Experiencer will be released from this impasse and go on to find a real solution.

Line 5
Things are taking a turn for the worse and the Experiencer will have to find a way to take action. He/she will need to go to someone in authority who has the power to deal with the problem. This strategy will have success and the danger can be averted.

Line 6
The Experiencer has achieved his/her goal, but is now entering

new territory. He/she will need to take time to study an unfamiliar situation and try to avoid the pitfalls that lay ahead. The Experiencer will have to find ways to consolidate his/her current position before any further moves can be made. It will be essential to establish contacts with reliable people and avoid those who are only acting out of self-interest.

8

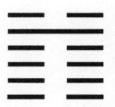

Unity

This hexagram represents *Unity* amongst people. It also points to a major effort to find and experience *Unity* with people. However, an idealistic search to link up with people who are engaged in meaningful work beyond the limitations of mere self-interest can develop into a curious journey with an ever-elusive destination.

Hexagram *Unity* is actually describing a pragmatic approach towards linking up with others, either by engaging in a practical relationship to achieve a concrete result, or by forming an alliance to overcome shared difficulties.

The Experiencer has the ability and stature to draw people together in a common enterprise, but may lack the material power to achieve this. If this is the case, the obvious option is to try to join an existing enterprise. The difficulty then lies in finding people who are genuinely open to outsiders and truly interested in those who wish to make a contribution.

Under the present circumstances the Experiencer will only succeed in arousing the interest of other people if they think it would be to their advantage. It is unlikely they will have any altruistic sentiments or any desire for friendship. Those who are enjoying security in their safe positions may not be inclined to show any interest in an outsider who is trying to link up with them. It would be a mistake to run around after people; they are either interested or not.

No matter how discouraging the situation may be, the Experiencer cannot afford to become confused and lose all sense of direction. The challenge is to keep an independent spirit and draw from one's own creative resources. With a strong sense of purpose and destiny the Experiencer will win through in the end.

The moving lines

Line 1
The Experiencer is trying to link up with others, but without success. This is a pity, because the Experiencer is sincere and has good intentions. Nevertheless, there will be a fortunate turn of events and help will come from unexpected quarters, enabling the Experiencer to overcome the current difficulties.

Line 2
The Experiencer is in a challenging situation and will need to keep to his/her principles at all costs. Any attempts to continue in this situation would only force the Experiencer into making regrettable compromises. The time has come to make preparations to leave. If the Experiencer moves carefully, he/she will be able to make a smooth exit.

Line 3
The Experiencer has linked up with the wrong kind of people and is now in a situation that is not leading anywhere. He/she will have to withdraw from this enterprise and find a different way to make progress.

Line 4

The Experiencer has the opportunity to link up with someone whom he/she holds in high esteem. This will become a mutually beneficial relationship which will prove to be invaluable for the longer term.

Line 5

The Experiencer is trying to link up with others, but should be prepared for disappointments along the way. If he/she is in contact with people who are proving to be unwilling or unhelpful, the Experiencer will just have to let them go.

Line 6

The Experiencer has linked up with people, but has arrived too late to achieve anything. Although there is no opportunity to have any real influence in this situation, it will nevertheless provide a secure position from which to consider options for the future.

The Power of Endurance

In this hexagram the I Ching uses the imagery of clouds moving across the sky, but the wind is blowing from a dry region and the clouds will bring no rain.

The Experiencer is able to draw from an inner source of creative energy. This ability gives the Experiencer the *Power of Endurance*. This power to endure is greatly needed now, because the Experiencer has little influence or status and there are no opportunities in sight. The times are difficult; many good and able people are marginalized, unable to act effectively in a society where moral values are fast losing their importance.

In the face of these adverse conditions the Experiencer is advised to be cautious and tread very carefully. He/she is in a weak position and cannot afford to make enemies. The challenge is to adapt to these restrictive circumstances and nevertheless make progress step by step. Clever diplomacy and a friendly manner will enable the Experiencer to maintain his/her current position and slowly work towards a future transition.

During this period the Experiencer will be able to find a way to develop and grow in the midst of a challenging era of wide-spread decline. This is a time to embark on creative projects, gradually developing skills and expertise in any area one is attracted to. Anything inspiring can be explored and developed. Progress will be slow, but the Experiencer will be able to assemble the building blocks for the future, never losing the belief that this preparatory work will eventually bear fruit.

The moving lines

Line 1

Progress is not possible now; there is limited scope to take action. The Experiencer is isolated and is facing serious opposition. He/she is advised to step back and make an effort to get a better grasp of what is really happening in the situation. This will make it possible to develop an effective strategy to deal with the current difficulties.

Line 2

The Experiencer has been considering a certain line of action, but is in doubt, because it would involve having to compromise his/her principles. Furthermore, it is very likely that such an initiative would lead to nothing. Therefore the Experiencer decides to withdraw and look for other ways to make progress.

Line 3

The Experiencer has aggressively pushed forward in an attempt to make progress, but this attempt has backfired. Nothing has been achieved; on the contrary, relations have been badly damaged and everything has ground to a halt. Instead of trying to force progress the Experiencer will have to find a way to convince people.

Line 4

The Experiencer is faced with a difficult and threatening situation. Nevertheless, with strength and confidence he/she will be able to overcome the problems without making any mistakes. The Experiencer's sincerity and good intentions will win through in the end.

Line 5

The Experiencer is willing to work for the common good and is in a position to use his/her talents to make a major contribution to the situation. The Experiencer's obvious sincerity and unselfish intentions will win the support of others.

Line 6

The Experiencer has achieved everything possible in the present situation. It is now essential to be content with the current state of affairs and not try to make any further progress. Any attempts to make more gains during this period would fail in a disastrous way. But a time will come when the Experiencer will need to look beyond the current circumstances for new opportunities.

10

Treading Correctly

In *Treading Correctly* the I Ching uses the image of a person stepping on the tail of a tiger without getting bitten.

This hexagram is about following the path of fate and destiny through risky circumstances to eventually emerge unscathed. It heralds a time of transition, of moving from location to location with a strong and resolute purpose in mind. On this path it is absolutely necessary to follow a clear aim in spite of the risks and difficulties involved in such an undertaking.

The Experiencer will be in situations where he/she will have to cope with unreasonable attitudes, stubborn behavior or worse. The issue of correct personal conduct in relation to dealing with difficult people is crucial here; a friendly but firm diplomatic profile must be maintained at all times. In this way the Experiencer will earn a reputation for being fair-minded and reasonable. This will be particularly helpful when dealing with people of influence, because the Experiencer will need to win their support in order to achieve his/her aim.

If the Experiencer treads correctly through these unfavorable circumstances, he/she will gradually succeed in discarding people and situations that are of no worth. Progress will be made by making contact with influential people or organizations, which can help the Experiencer to achieve his/her aims. A successful transition will be the outcome.

The moving lines

Line 1
The Experiencer should abandon any ambitions in the present situation and follow an independent path. This is the only way to avoid coming into conflict with others. By choosing a direction that is in accordance with his/her deepest wishes the Experiencer will be able to follow the path of destiny.

Line 2
The Experiencer lives modestly and is sincerely following a path of personal development. The Experiencer will not go astray, because he/she is not attracted to worldly success for its own sake. This is the way to make progress on the path of destiny.

Line 3
The Experiencer has seriously overestimated his/her abilities and is pushing forward recklessly into danger. He/she is not aware of the serious difficulties around the corner. This course of action will lead to failure and the Experiencer will suffer damage as a result.

Line 4
The Experiencer is in a very challenging situation in which everything could go completely wrong. In order to avoid complete failure it will be essential to obtain the support of people in authority. If the Experiencer treads carefully, he/she will succeed in winning their trust. This will eventually lead to a major breakthrough.

Line 5
The Experiencer has the strength to come to grips with the

current difficulties and act decisively. This is very necessary, because a resolute attitude is the only way to deal with a very unsatisfactory situation. The Experiencer is warned to be constantly mindful of the risks involved and maintain a certain degree of caution.

Line 6

The Experiencer is sincere and has acted correctly at all times. As a result he/she has succeeded in building up warm and friendly relations with positive and constructive people. The Experiencer can now reap the harvest of his/her efforts and achieve a real success.

11

Peace

This hexagram represents a period of peace and harmony, a time of contentment and accomplishment. It is almost as though the gods have conspired to create a season of happiness. Everything runs like a train, smoothly and consistently, and completely on track. The Experiencer has the energy and the creativity to engage in important projects which have the potential to bring about lasting fulfillment. Everything that is sown during this period can be harvested for many years to come. This is also a harmonious time in which close relationships flourish, giving joy and strength day after day.

The time of *Peace* will eventually wane and circumstances will change. Therefore it is important to use the opportunities the time of *Peace* offers, while it lasts.

This can be illustrated by the following two scenarios.

In the first scenario the Experiencer is engaged in meaningful and often exhilarating work in a very sociable setting. The daily activity in the workplace brings people together into stimulating relationships, creating friendship and happiness in an atmosphere of mutual support. Everything is in harmony and there is no conflict between people; a time of *Peace* is ushered in. However, the situation will not last. The wrong people will worm their way into positions of authority, the equilibrium will be disturbed, and harmony will be destroyed. This development will force the Experiencer to leave the situation.

In the second scenario the Experiencer reaches a destination that has a healing and deeply beneficial quality. After a period of struggle and misfortune the Experiencer has arrived, at last, in a beautifully peaceful and relaxing place. A happy and carefree time follows, creating the conditions for a significant personal development. It will be a fruitful and very important period in the Experiencer's life, but it will not last. People who have power over the Experiencer's circumstances will be unable to maintain the equilibrium of *Peace* and things will start to fall apart, forcing the Experiencer to flee.

The moving lines

Line 1
The time is coming closer when a major transition can be made. The Experiencer is prepared to make a long journey and leave behind an old lifestyle that has lost its momentum. He/she will succeed in embarking on a new way of life.

Line 2
Progress is no longer possible in the present situation. The Experiencer has to cope with selfish or downright uncivilized people. He/she is almost completely isolated and the time has come to look towards the future. Eventually a transition will have to be made, but it will not be achieved quickly or easily. The Experiencer is faced with the challenging prospect of making a journey to a new destination with limited means. This is a difficult fate, but the Experiencer will be able to continue on his/her quest, never losing sight of the ultimate goal of achieving fulfillment.

Line 3

The Experiencer has achieved success and is living in very pleasant circumstances. However, the Experiencer is warned that the good times will not last and a recession will be inevitable. One should enjoy the good times while they last, but be prepared for the downturn when it comes. If the Experiencer is mindful of this, he/she will be able to take the necessary measures in time.

Line 4

The Experiencer is prepared to offer his/her abilities in the service of others. People will recognize the Experiencer's good intentions and be pleased to accept his/her offer. The Experiencer will be able to cooperate with others in an open and sincere way, and work on a project for the common good.

Line 5

The Experiencer is enjoying a time of prosperity and relationships are flourishing. His/her generosity and willingness to reach out to others will enable the Experiencer to team up with people and lay the foundation for something that will bear fruit in the future.

Line 6

The situation is coming to an end. It is no longer possible to prevent this. The Experiencer is urged to come to terms with the reality; any plans to save the situation will come to nothing. The Experiencer will have to hold on with strength and dignity until an opportunity comes to make a transition.

12

Standstill

Standstill ushers in a time of exile and isolation.

Egoistic, self-serving people have penetrated into positions of power, forcing the Experiencer to step aside. When mediocrity rules it is impossible for the Experiencer to make any progress and the only option left is to give up on the situation and walk away. This is a life-changing experience. It means leaving behind a familiar world that has become damaged, actually tainted by the unpleasantness of negative people. By choosing to follow a truly individual path the Experiencer will enter a new phase in life, a period of self-imposed exile.

The serious implications of exile soon become apparent. Alone and empty-handed, the Experiencer has to cope, without friends or connections, with very challenging circumstances. Day after day the Experiencer searches for opportunities to find a way out of isolation, but all of these efforts are in vain. Nothing happens and life comes to a standstill.

At this point in time the Experiencer is advised to step back and stop trying to make societal progress. There is a great risk that history will repeat itself and the Experiencer would once again find him/herself in the company of mediocre people who have become corrupted by power. Any ambitious attempts to engage in societal activity at this time could seriously compromise the Experiencer's integrity. It would also be extremely difficult to find recognition anywhere.

Paradoxically, when the doors of the outer world are closed, the doors of the inner world will begin to open. The Experiencer can start to focus on the deeper meaning of his/her life and develop a vision for the future.

Sooner or later there will be a change for the better and the doors of the outer world will begin to open again. The Experiencer can then start to work on a plan to transition out of the place of *Standstill*.

The moving lines

Line 1

The Experiencer is advised to step back and try to avoid any further involvement in the current situation. This is the only way to avoid making regrettable compromises. Now is not the time to take any initiatives; the Experiencer should wait and allow events to run their course. The right way forward will gradually become clear.

Line 2

The Experiencer is in a situation where petty and mediocre people have the upper hand. He/she is advised to take a distance from these people; otherwise a serious conflict will become unavoidable. In this way the Experiencer can maintain his/her integrity and dignity.

Line 3

Mediocre and incompetent people are in positions of power and the Experiencer is completely marginalized. When the Experiencer decides to stop his/her involvement and retreat from the situation, they will feel ashamed.

Line 4
The time has come to find a way out of standstill. The Experiencer has reached a crossroads and will need to choose a new direction in life.

Line 5
The Experiencer is trying to find a way out of a situation of standstill, but is gradually discovering that his/her present plans are impossible to achieve. An insight into the true nature of the situation enables the Experiencer to develop a realistic plan of action, which will eventually succeed. However, this plan will require careful preparation and a sustained effort to keep it on track.

Line 6
The Experiencer is trying to find a way out of a situation of standstill through making important contacts with influential people. With their help it will be possible to solve a long-standing problem, but this will not bring an end to the present stagnation. Nevertheless, it will put the Experiencer in a better position to look for an opportunity to get out of standstill.

13

Fellowship (Mutual Cooperation)
Fellowship represents the Experiencer's search to find people of like kind, kindred spirits, who share the same level of awareness.

This hexagram has two possible scenarios which are indirectly related to one another.

In the first scenario the Experiencer is embarking on a search for fellowship. He/she may be living in isolation in humble circumstances, seeking friendship and purpose in an otherwise meaningless world. But the search for fellowship is a long and difficult experience, sometimes leading to the doorsteps of deceptive people and secretive cliques, who have wrapped themselves in the cloak of fellowship and good intentions. The Experiencer will be confronted with the selfishness of those who claim the moral high ground, but do not truly live their ideals.

In the second scenario the Experiencer is given an opportunity to cooperate with others in a mutually supportive way. It is very much in the interest of the Experiencer to make a commitment to team up with people during this period, even though the relationships are only based on utility and lack the depth of lasting friendship.

Fellowship is a time of encounters. When the Experiencer

succeeds in joining a fellowship, he/she will be welcomed and enjoy good friendship. But in an imperfect world nothing really lasts. Sooner or later the Experiencer will have to deal with people who have selfish motives and hidden agendas, and then the happiness of fellowship will turn into disappointment. When this happens the Experiencer will need to find a new direction and move on.

The moving lines

Line 1
The Experiencer is trying to join up with others in fellowship. He/she approaches a group of people in a sincere and open-minded way, hoping to be accepted into the group. The Experiencer soon realizes that it will not be possible to find fellowship with these people and decides to withdraw.

Line 2
The Experiencer is trying to join up with others in fellowship. Unfortunately, the group the Experiencer is trying to join is a self-interested clique which does not welcome outsiders. In fact, this group does not represent true fellowship at all. It would be a mistake to persevere in this, because the Experiencer will certainly be rejected.

Line 3
The Experiencer is trying to join up with others in fellowship, but is only meeting with distrust and opposition. The people he/she is trying to deal with are small-minded and suspicious, and certainly do not represent the spirit of fellowship. The Experiencer is advised to accept this unfortunate turn of events and cease contact with these people.

Line 4

The Experiencer is trying to join up with others in fellowship, but cannot come to an agreement with them. In fact, the negotiations have led to a stalemate. The Experiencer is advised to give up on this attempt and withdraw to consider other ways to make progress. This will make it possible to find the right way ahead.

Line 5

After a long period of difficulties and struggle the Experiencer can finally unite with friends in true fellowship. The result will be a friendship that can stand the test of time.

Line 6

The Experiencer has succeeded in linking up with others, but the friendship is superficial and unsatisfying. A relationship with these people will be short-lived, because it lacks any lasting significance. At this point the Experiencer will face the challenge of having to make a drastic change in his/her life.

14

Great Personal Resources
This hexagram represents creative energy and clarity of mind.

The Experiencer has the energy, the ability, and the material resources to make a major transition. A clear sense of purpose and a bold plan will enable the Experiencer to go ahead and make the right moves at the right time. The Experiencer's strong motivation will make it possible to achieve whatever needs to be undertaken, no matter how impossible it may appear to be. With a positive and constructive attitude the Experiencer will be able to attract help and support from other people to carry out his/her plan.

Dealing correctly with a problematic situation will be instrumental in winning through the current difficulties. The Experiencer's excellent sense of timing will ensure that he/she can keep abreast of developments and act decisively when the time is ripe. By acting in time the Experiencer will be able to prevent any wrongdoers from becoming disruptive or causing irreparable damage. Nobody will have the power to block the Experiencer's progress. His/her honest intentions and strength of character will win the goodwill and appreciation of those who are in positions of authority. And as a result, the Experiencer will receive all the help and support needed to make a smooth exit from difficult circumstances.

A successful breakthrough into a new, more fulfilling situation will be the outcome.

The moving lines

Line 1

The Experiencer is making a new start in an unfamiliar situation. He/she is strong and resourceful and can confidently embark on a new period in life. The Experiencer will not make any mistakes, providing he/she is aware of the dangers and pitfalls of the situation. By keeping a distance from people who are potentially harmful the Experiencer will be able to stay out of trouble.

Line 2

The Experiencer is strong and resourceful. He/she has the staying power to succeed, but also the ability to move on, if it becomes necessary to do so. The Experiencer will not make any mistakes, because he/she has the clarity of mind to know when to persevere in an undertaking or when to step out and look for something else.

Line 3

The Experiencer is fair-minded and willing to generously provide resources to benefit others. The Experiencer will need to carefully choose the people he/she can benefit and avoid those who are not worthwhile.

Line 4

The Experiencer is strong and resourceful, but will have to tread carefully in the present circumstances. He/she is advised to be impartial and independent, because there may be a temptation to take sides, which would be a mistake. The Experiencer should maintain his/her independence and integrity by keeping a distance from petty jealousies and conflicts.

Line 5

This is a time to be confident in one's ability to inspire others to cooperate. The Experiencer's sincerity and unpretentiousness will win the sympathy and support of other people. He/she has the stature and authority to convince or impress people whenever necessary.

Line 6

The Experiencer is not focused on material success. He/she is working on something of quality and beauty that will have a lasting power to inspire people. The Experiencer's work will inevitably meet with recognition.

15

Modesty

Hexagram *Modesty* represents cosmic or natural justice, whereby over time everyone will reap the harvest they have sown and receive their just deserts accordingly.

Modesty also represents an attitude which understands and accepts the power of cosmic justice.

The Experiencer is suffering an injustice of some kind and as a result is living under restrictive circumstances. Trying to make any progress in life is proving to be frustrating and very challenging. *Modesty* begins with accepting the outcome of events, even though things have turned out to be far from perfect. Accepting the reality as it actually is should not be confused with fatalism; it simply means understanding that nothing more can be achieved under the present circumstances. The Experiencer will have to come to terms with the situation and accept the reality as it is, no matter how disappointing things are.

It is essential to practice self-restraint in the face of the current difficulties. There is a danger of being drawn into unpleasant confrontations with arrogant or mediocre people. It is very important to keep a low profile and react cautiously to any events; this is the only way to maintain a relatively secure position in a potentially volatile situation. As events unfold, the Experiencer will be able to see what the various players are doing, both to themselves and others, and from this perspective he/she will come to understand that they will all get their just deserts in the end.

The time of *Modesty* creates depth of character and the ability to succeed through patience and perseverance. When the Experiencer is ready to look beyond the current situation in search of opportunities, the way forward will open up. In the end everything will fall into place and the Experiencer will be released from these restrictive circumstances.

The moving lines

Line 1

The Experiencer is in a lowly position and has very little power or influence. By being modest and correct the Experiencer will be able to avoid getting into difficulties with people. As a result it will be possible to accomplish whatever needs to be undertaken in a quiet and diplomatic way.

Line 2

The Experiencer has the strength of character to persevere on a slow and difficult path, gradually achieving his/her aims. By being modest and sincere the Experiencer will succeed in winning the trust of others.

Line 3

The Experiencer enjoys a certain status, but does not boast or act in an arrogant manner. By remaining modest and correct he/she will win the appreciation and the support of others. In this way a spirit of cooperation can be established and the Experiencer will be able to accomplish his/her aims.

Line 4
If the Experiencer is realistic and not overambitious, mistakes can be avoided and everything will gradually fall into place.

Line 5
The Experiencer is confronted with the necessity to take strong action to resolve a serious problem. Nevertheless, this must be done in a just and correct manner. By being modest and reasonable it will be possible to win the support of others and succeed.

Line 6
This is a time of reflection. The Experiencer will need to adopt a modest and completely realistic attitude in order to make an honest assessment of his/her hopes and ambitions. As a result the Experiencer will be able to look at the situation with fresh eyes and come with a different approach.

16

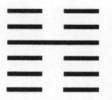

Enthusiasm

The Experiencer has entered a situation with energy and optimism only to encounter serious obstacles and difficulties. All attempts to push forward singlehandedly have ended in failure and disillusionment. In fact, the situation has turned out to be more problematic and complicated than the Experiencer imagined.

At this point the Experiencer should seek out allies, who can be of real assistance in finding a way through the difficulties. Once the Experiencer realizes that nothing can be achieved without help, the way forward will start to open up. By adopting a constructive and flexible approach the Experiencer will succeed in winning the support of others to overcome the current problems. This will have the effect of drawing people together to achieve a shared purpose. It will then be possible to fulfill an important task in a very challenging situation. The Experiencer will emerge stronger and wiser as a result of this process.

The aftermath of *Enthusiasm* is always a great feeling of accomplishment, but the feeling of enthusiasm will not last. Whatever success has been achieved will be limited and relatively short-lived. Obstacles still remain and the Experiencer will have to be very persevering to make any further progress, otherwise an increasing feeling of disillusionment could lead to inertia.

The moving lines

Line 1

The Experiencer is enthusiastically trying to achieve a breakthrough, but does not succeed due to an unfortunate turn of events. This outcome is completely unexpected, leaving the Experiencer shocked and deeply disappointed.

Line 2

The Experiencer is realistic and very aware of the beginnings of a serious deterioration in the situation. He/she can see the crisis coming and therefore decides to wait no longer. The Experiencer will immediately take the necessary measures to organize his/her retreat from the situation.

Line 3

The Experiencer is very enthusiastic about a proposal from people who seem to offer a real opportunity to make progress. He/she will eventually regret becoming too dependent on these people, because their proposals will turn out to be of little substance. Nevertheless, the current circumstances do offer a window of opportunity, but only if the Experiencer is realistic and prepared to follow an independent path.

Line 4

The Experiencer is enthusiastically pursuing an aim or working on an important project. This will become a prolonged and difficult effort and will take a long time to succeed. It will not be possible to speed things up, because events must be allowed to unfold at their own pace. Inevitably, the Experiencer will feel discouraged along the way; the Experiencer should nevertheless have no doubt that he/she will eventually succeed in attracting the help and enthusiasm of others to complete his/her endeavor.

Line 5

The Experiencer is suffering harassment from people who are trying to force him/her out of the situation. They will not succeed, because the Experiencer is perfectly capable of fending off any attacks. The Experiencer will be able to stand his/her ground and win through in the end.

Line 6

Blinded by enthusiasm, the Experiencer is following an unrealistic course of action that is not going to succeed. Fortunately, the Experiencer will see his/her mistake in time and abandon this plan.

Guided by Events

This hexagram refers to the art of following the flow of events with an alert and watchful intelligence, capable of acting decisively when the time is ripe. This could involve travel, or a long distance transition.

In a major effort to overcome his/her current difficulties the Experiencer is actively searching for solutions. However, trying to force the course of events at this time would be unwise and unnecessary; events will take a turn for the better, although in a surprising way. The Experiencer will need to reconsider any cherished ideas or preferences, because the solution will be found in an unexpected place and could easily be overlooked. Therefore it is very important not to dismiss anything that may seem to be second best.

For the time being the Experiencer will need to adapt to the situation as it is, until the way forward becomes clear. It is important to take time to withdraw and rest whenever possible, and not waste energy by getting drawn into any intrigues in the current situation. If the Experiencer can let go and allow events to run their course, his/her feelings of stress and anxiety will diminish.

It is very important to develop a sense of timing and wait until things fall into place. When change starts to gather pace, the Experiencer will see the way to act. Everything depends upon seizing the moment when the right time comes. This will succeed.

The moving lines

Line 1
The time has come to change course. The Experiencer's outlook on life has evolved and therefore his/her aims are changing. By becoming more open-minded the Experiencer will reconsider possibilities previously discarded as second best. The Experiencer is a free agent and has the power to put the finger on the right solution. This will succeed.

Line 2
The Experiencer has chosen to stay within his/her comfort zone, but the joy will be short-lived. Staying within the realm of the familiar will only curtail the Experiencer's development as an independent individual.

Line 3
The Experiencer is presented with a choice. He/she can remain in the present situation or take a risk and enter unknown territory. If the Experiencer decides to step out of his/her comfort zone, it will be possible to follow a truly independent path. This is very challenging, but the Experiencer should be steadfast in carrying out this decision. This path will lead to discovering the deeper purpose of one's life.

Line 4
The Experiencer is searching for a way of life that is true to his/her ideals. He/she succeeds in making contact with people who claim to represent many of these ideals in the work they

are doing. Unfortunately, it gradually becomes clear that they are not completely genuine. The Experiencer is advised to cease contact with these people and follow an independent path.

Line 5

The Experiencer is prepared to follow the path of destiny, even though this means leaving the familiar behind and stepping into the unknown. Events are going to take a surprising turn and fate will lead the Experiencer to a completely unexpected destination.

Line 6

The Experiencer has made plans to retire. However, as a result of an unexpected event he/she is drawn back into the world of activity. There still remains an important task the Experiencer is fated to engage in.

18

Work on What Others Have Spoiled

The situation has completely failed to come up to expectations. Time passes by, but there are no positive developments. An intense feeling of disappointment is leading to depression and lethargy. Everything drifts on, indecisiveness creeps in, and the Experiencer starts to lose his/her sense of purpose. The time has come to get a grip on the present state of affairs. The Experiencer is in a position to penetrate into the deeper meaning of these challenging circumstances and draw some very important conclusions.

This disappointing experience has its roots in the past, because the situation has been spoiled by other people long before the Experiencer arrived. Those in positions of authority have neglected their duty by failing to deal with the negative elements responsible for the current decline.

The Experiencer cannot shoulder the burden of responsibility for things that have been ruined by others. However, he/she can make the relevant people aware of what has been spoiled. It may be possible, to some degree, to improve the situation, but it is far more important for the Experiencer to regain the momentum in his/her life. Developing a new purpose will reinvigorate the Experiencer and inspire him/her to take action. This will lead to a decision to give up on the current situation and move on.

The moving lines

Line 1

The Experiencer is confronted with a situation which has been spoiled by others. It will be possible to work on what has been spoiled, but there is a limit to what can be achieved. If the Experiencer has a realistic view of the situation and is aware of the pitfalls, he/she will eventually succeed in making some improvements.

Line 2

The Experiencer is confronted with a situation which has been spoiled by others. The atmosphere is poisoned by negative and spiteful attitudes which have thoroughly spoilt relations. The Experiencer is not in a position to change or influence the attitudes of these people. He/she will have to withdraw and consider other ways to make progress.

Line 3

The Experiencer is working on what has been spoiled by others. He/she has approached the current problems in a strong and energetic way, but has been overconfident. The Experiencer is advised to step back and try to gain a better understanding of the situation. Serious mistakes can be avoided by acting in a careful and diplomatic manner.

Line 4

The Experiencer is confronted with a situation which has been spoiled by others, but should not get involved in this. To do so would be a serious mistake. This is a time to focus on personal development and find a way to make a new start.

Line 5

The Experiencer is in a position to work on what has been

spoiled by others. He/she will be able to make a stand against corruption and abuses of power, and convince the authorities to implement some reforms. However, a complete overhaul of the situation will not be possible, because the Experiencer will come up against the limits of what can be achieved.

Line 6
The Experiencer does not need to work on what has been spoiled. He/she can withdraw and follow a higher aim.

Approach

Hexagram *Approach* points to a time of good fortune, but misfortune will follow and cannot be avoided. This hexagram refers to a cyclic phenomenon; a time of growth leading to recession and a time of recession leading to growth.

Approach represents the culmination of favorable conditions that will enable the Experiencer to engage successfully in the field of activity. This is the start of a very productive period in which significant achievements can be made. The Experiencer will be in a position to team up with others, often in challenging circumstances, in a major effort to change a situation for the better. This will have success. However, it is very important to take advantage of this success to consolidate one's position and establish a solid reputation while the good times last. Social contacts and strong relationships will prove to be invaluable in the time to come. Allies will be indispensable to help guard against the negative and destructive tendencies of others when conditions start to deteriorate.

Approach shows a supremely intelligent response to the cyclic phenomenon of positive and negative change in the outer world. When things take a turn for the worse, the Experiencer will be in a strong position to ride out the period of misfortune.

The moving lines

Line 1
The Experiencer is in a position to team up with allies in a bid to overcome the current difficulties. A joint effort to come to grips with a negative situation will have a powerful impact. The Experiencer and his/her allies will have to work hard to consolidate their success while the good times last.

Line 2
The Experiencer can team up with others and make significant progress during this period. However, a recession will be unavoidable. When the recession hits, the Experiencer will be able to withdraw in time.

Line 3
The Experiencer has been overconfident in his/her dealings with others and this is having a negative effect on the situation. If the Experiencer starts dealing with people in a more honest and straightforward way, it will be possible to mend relations. This will open the way for a period of growth and flourishing relationships.

Line 4
The Experiencer's success has reached its peak. The situation is slowly starting to decline, but this is not the fault of the Experiencer; a recession is inevitable and cannot be prevented. The Experiencer will have to accept that the good times will not last and realize that this period in his/her life is coming to an end.

Line 5
When the recession comes it will usher in a time of limitations. Fortunately, the Experiencer is capable of coping with

increasingly restrictive circumstances, because he/she is realistic and adaptable.

Line 6

The recession is coming to an end and opportunities will be opening up again. By honestly and generously offering his/her skills and talents the Experiencer will be able to get back into business. This will be a complete success.

20

The View

In this hexagram the I Ching uses the image of a tower, which offers the Experiencer a perfect view of the entire surroundings.

The View represents a vantage point, a place where the Experiencer can review the past and think about possibilities for the future. It is possible that an event or activity from the Experiencer's past will become relevant again and be of great significance for the future. Alternatively, a radically new initiative could open up a completely different way of life.

The Experiencer has arrived at a crossroads and will now have to consider which direction to take. This will not be easy. A lot of time and effort will have to be spent on finding the right way forward. From the present vantage point the Experiencer has a complete overview of the outside world. This will enable the Experiencer to make an accurate and penetrating assessment of the present state of affairs and consider potential opportunities beyond the current situation.

The View ushers in a period of contemplation, in which the Experiencer can explore the deeper meaning underlying past events and experiences in his/her life. It is also a period of enquiry and preliminary research in order to evaluate concrete possibilities and find a way to make progress. The Experiencer can pursue any area that is in tune with his/her path of development and eventually make a leap forward. Any insights or knowledge gained during this period of contemplation and enquiry will give the Experiencer the power to have a real influence, both in the present situation and in relation to making contacts elsewhere.

The moving lines

Line 1
The Experiencer has reached a vantage point, but is failing to use this opportunity to make an objective assessment of the situation. He/she will need to gain a thorough and realistic understanding of how to make progress in a difficult and complex environment.

Line 2
The Experiencer has reached a vantage point, but is failing to look beyond the narrow confines of his/her own viewpoint. The time has come to see oneself in relation to others and try to anticipate what actions they will take; otherwise the Experiencer could be on the receiving end of some unpleasant surprises.

Line 3
The Experiencer has reached a crossroads. From the present vantage point he/she will be able to review the past and make an objective assessment of possible options for the future. This will enable the Experiencer to choose a realistic goal and start working gradually towards it.

Line 4
From the present vantage point the Experiencer can see the extent of a serious and widespread decline. For this reason he/she is in a position to give advice to those who are in power. It is

essential that the Experiencer maintains his/her independence by only playing the role of a temporary advisor.

Line 5

From the present vantage point the Experiencer can review the past and understand the underlying motives that have guided his/her choices. This process of self-reflection enables the Experiencer to focus on the things that truly have meaning in his/her life. As a result the Experiencer will decide to give up on a situation that has turned stale and venture into something new.

Line 6

From the present vantage point the Experiencer can look deeply into the past. A summing up of everything that has gone before can now take place. It will become clear that the Experiencer's desire to join up with others in meaningful activity is still unfulfilled.

Making a Judgment

Making a Judgment represents a robust and sustained effort to find out if something is of any worth. The Experiencer is determined to find out the truth about things and shed light on whatever obstacles are blocking progress. This will enable the Experiencer to make a clear judgment of the situation and decide whether to continue or not.

In an all-out bid to find a solution for a serious problem the Experiencer has become entangled in a situation that is not leading anywhere. Winning the approval and cooperation of people in authority is proving to be extremely difficult. The Experiencer's proposals are genuine and completely realistic; unfortunately, those who have the power to make a decision on this matter are inflexible and stubborn, preferring to follow their own ideas and prejudices.

As a result progress has ground to a halt. The Experiencer will have to abandon any idea of reaching a solution in the present situation. This is a great disappointment, because the Experiencer had been convinced a breakthrough could be achieved. At this point the Experiencer will have to cut through the knot and make a clear and rational decision. The time has come to move on.

The obstacles the Experiencer is facing cannot be easily overcome.

Nevertheless, *Making a Judgment* represents a significant experience, because it is the beginning of an important process of elimination which will eventually yield a solution.

The moving lines

Line 1
The Experiencer is seriously considering an ambitious plan of action, but this would be a big mistake. Fortunately, a turn of events prevents the Experiencer from carrying out this plan. As time progresses the Experiencer will realize he/she has narrowly avoided taking a disastrous course of action. This will lead to a totally new insight into the situation.

Line 2
The Experiencer is taking drastic action to chastise a person who is acting in a completely unethical way. Although the Experiencer's action is very robust, it is not a mistake. He/she is meting out a just punishment which puts an end to the disgraceful behavior of someone who has repeatedly done wrong.

Line 3
In an attempt to correct an injustice the Experiencer meets with resistance and anger. He/she is not in a very strong position and is getting involved in a very unpleasant situation with a long and unsavory history. The Experiencer will eventually realize that he/she does not have the power to achieve a just solution in this situation and will decide to pull out.

Line 4
The Experiencer is confronting a powerful opponent and is meeting with strong resistance. The Experiencer will have to make a sound judgment of the situation and then decide if it is

21

worthwhile to persevere with this effort.

Line 5

The situation is not immediately clear. The Experiencer cannot arrive at a judgment until all the facts are available. He/she cannot afford to make a judgment based on appearances, because there will be hidden surprises. The Experiencer is advised to step back and allow events to unfold before making a final judgment.

Line 6

The Experiencer has been following a disaster course. He/she has completely misjudged the situation and is failing to see the danger signs. If the Experiencer continues in this way, it will result in misfortune.

109

22

Authenticity

Authenticity ushers in a period in which the Experiencer is challenged to be for real and follow a truly authentic path through life. If the Experiencer has lost the way or made an error of judgment, now is the time to regain clarity of mind and find the right way forward. The journey must go on.

Things have not turned out well. A situation that had seemed to be a bona fide opportunity for a good and positive experience has become a major disappointment. Appearances can be so very deceptive. In reality the Experiencer had entered an arena in which the key players are neither genuine nor honest. Their inflated sense of self-importance and desire for status can be destructive and could easily damage whatever is true and authentic. In such a situation it is impossible for the Experiencer to make any progress. The moment will soon come when the Experiencer decides to confront these people face to face and question the sincerity of their motives. However, the Experiencer lacks the power to force through any changes. He/she does not have the authority to make decisions on important issues in this situation.

This is a very challenging experience, because there are no easy solutions and the way out will be difficult to find. As events unfold the Experiencer will come to realize that the current predicament is part of a pattern of recurring experiences in his/her life. This has all happened before. It will take a major effort to break free and leave these experiences behind forever. The only way forward is to follow a path with a heart, even if this means taking risks and travelling to unknown destinations. Embarking on a quest, a magical journey of discovery, will eventually reveal the Experiencer's true mission in life.

The moving lines

Line 1

The Experiencer has reached a dead end and is trying to find a way to make progress. He/she will have to follow an independent path and not become dependent on any groups or organizations. In this way the Experiencer will stay true to his/her principles and be able to live a life that is for real.

Line 2

There is no easy way out of the present standstill. The Experiencer will need strength and patience to cope with a situation in which he/she has little power or influence. Nevertheless, the Experiencer's sincerity and strength of character will earn the respect of others.

Line 3

The Experiencer has arrived in an idyllic situation, but is in danger of becoming mesmerized and seduced by its charm. It would be a mistake to try to stay here, because this would only lead to stagnation. The Experiencer is encouraged to persevere in following an authentic path and continue the search for truly meaningful opportunities.

Line 4

The Experiencer has a choice to remain in a comfortable but

stagnant situation or step out of it to follow a path of simplicity and authenticity. He/she will have a sudden encounter, which will turn out to be surprisingly beneficial. This encounter will inspire the Experiencer to make the right choices and follow an authentic purpose in life.

Line 5

The Experiencer has engaged in an effort to make material gains, but this has turned into a complete failure. However, nothing has been lost. The way is open to return to a truly authentic way of life. The Experiencer will find that it will not be necessary to worry about earning material rewards, because this will happen spontaneously as a result of conscientious and consistent work.

Line 6

The Experiencer is trying to follow a path of truth and authenticity in very restrictive circumstances. A spirit of independence will be needed to keep one's inner light burning in times of adversity. Over time the Experiencer will succeed in rediscovering his/her mission in life, eventually becoming free of regret despite having experienced misfortune.

23

Collapse

The situation is deteriorating and will eventually become unsustainable. The people in positions of authority are stubborn and incompetent and their emotional judgments result in serious abuses of power. The few good and able people who remain here are marginalized or seriously restricted.

The Experiencer will have to accept that there is no future here. There is nothing he/she can do about it. It would be a mistake to become emotionally involved in this situation; the Experiencer would only become entangled in an increasingly pointless and unpleasant experience. It is better to keep a distance from the spiteful and mediocre people who are dominating the situation.

Nevertheless, there is no easy way out of this predicament, because there are very few options available. It would be premature to try to take any initiatives at this stage; events will have to run their course. A point will be reached when the situation begins to fall apart and the Experiencer's position becomes untenable. When the collapse gathers momentum and reaches a climax, the Experiencer will see the way out and break free.

The moving lines

Line 1
Petty, hostile people are secretly scheming to undermine the Experiencer's position. Through gossip and intrigue they seek to destroy the reputation of the Experiencer and his/her allies. A point will be reached when the Experiencer's opponents will make an open bid to force him/her out. The Experiencer will realize that it will not be possible to prevent this. It will only be a matter of time until he/she is forced to leave the situation.

Line 2
The Experiencer is underestimating the seriousness of the situation. He/she is in a precarious position without any allies. Trying to continue in the present circumstances would be a big mistake; the situation is sooner or later going to fall apart. The Experiencer is strongly advised to become realistic and devise an exit strategy before it is too late.

Line 3
The situation is going from bad to worse and the Experiencer's relations with others are falling apart. This is not the Experiencer's fault. The time has come to withdraw and consider other ways to make progress.

Line 4
The collapse of the current situation is imminent. The Experiencer is urged to see the situation as it really is and focus on finding a way out; otherwise the Experiencer will be overtaken by events.

Line 5
The Experiencer is in a precarious position. Fortunately, his/her good character and reliability will win the goodwill of others. This will enable the Experiencer to gain a secure foothold in the

situation and establish a vantage point from which to search for better opportunities.

Line 6

The Experiencer will be given a golden opportunity to leave a situation which is on the verge of collapse. Those who have lived selfishly, never reaching out to others, will not be able to avoid the collapse; they will be ruined. The Experiencer will be able to use his/her resources to make a new start elsewhere.

24

Return

Return symbolizes the time of the winter solstice, when everything is withdrawn until the return of the light and the approach of spring. The need to withdraw and take time for reflection until a way is found to return to the flow of life is the essential meaning of this hexagram.

An important aspect of *Return* is doing the right thing at the right time. The Experiencer withdraws at the right time to avoid making unnecessary mistakes and returns to the world of activity when the time is ripe.

There are three different scenarios in this hexagram and in each one the Experiencer is forced to withdraw from a situation that has become unsustainable.

In the first scenario the destructive impact of a major setback is bringing to an end a successful period in the Experiencer's life. He/she has no choice but to withdraw and find a way to make a new start. In the second scenario the Experiencer has to withdraw from a deteriorating situation and face the prospect of having to make a major transition. In the third scenario the Experiencer is forced to withdraw from a mistaken effort to make progress, which has led nowhere. He/she has lost the way and will need a time of reflection to focus on finding a new direction in life.

Return ushers in a period of contemplation and rest. During this time the Experiencer will go through a process of personal growth and gain a deeper understanding of the recent events in his/her life, while gradually developing a clearer sense of direction. By reconnecting with the things that truly correspond with his/her spirit the Experiencer will build up the power to return to the world of activity and enter a new phase in life.

The moving lines

Line 1
The Experiencer is realizing that the present course of action is leading nowhere. Fortunately, this insight comes in time and it is still possible to turn back before it is too late. A genuine opportunity is just over the horizon.

Line 2
The Experiencer decides to change course and follow a new direction. As a consequence the Experiencer will withdraw from his/her current activity to engage in a completely different area. This move will usher in a period of growth and prosperity.

Line 3
The Experiencer is entering a very challenging period and there is no way of avoiding this. His/her path through life will lead in and out of misfortune, but somehow he/she will find the strength to continue against all the odds.

Line 4
The Experiencer has misjudged the situation and has become involved with the wrong people. As events unfold, the Experiencer will have an unpleasant surprise and discover that these people cannot be trusted. Realizing his/her mistake, the Experiencer will come to the decision to withdraw and follow

an independent path.

Line 5

The Experiencer has been following a wrong course of action in an effort to make progress in life. This has failed completely. Fortunately, the Experiencer realizes he/she has made a mistake and draws some important lessons from this experience. Sadder and wiser, the Experiencer now faces the challenge to search for an opportunity to make a new beginning.

Line 6

The Experiencer has been following a path which has led nowhere. As a result he/she is overcome by confusion. Continuing in this way will lead to exhaustion. A period of reflection will be needed to learn from past mistakes and find a new direction.

Following the Will of Heaven

Following the Will of Heaven means following a line of action that is in accordance with the Experiencer's destiny.

Setting out to accomplish something will only succeed if the Experiencer *follows the will of Heaven*. This means becoming aware of one's true purpose or mission in life and acting accordingly. Any deviation from the path of destiny will miss the mark and lead to misfortune.

In an effort to make progress the Experiencer is considering a plan of action that is ill-conceived. This would be a big mistake; any impulsive or premature action taken now could lead to serious difficulties. The Experiencer does not have a complete grasp of the situation and has no idea how things are going to develop. Therefore, it is very important to keep an open mind and allow events to unfold in their own way. To find a way to act decisively the Experiencer will need to step back and allow the situation to develop of its own accord. Events will take a surprising turn and the Experiencer will understand why his/her intended course of action would have been a big mistake. At this point the right way forward will become clear.

If the Experiencer succeeds in *following the will of Heaven*, he/she will enter a new episode in his/her life. It will usher in a time of sustained creative work and many accomplishments.

The moving lines

Line 1

Unconcerned about approval or recognition, the Experiencer is following his/her heart. This will eventually lead to good fortune.

Line 2

If the Experiencer does not try to force things, but allows events to run their course, he/she will be able to act at the right time and make a successful transition.

Line 3

The Experiencer has taken a wrong or premature initiative which has led to unexpected and unfortunate consequences. The Experiencer has failed to take into account the feelings of others and this has resulted in a backlash.

Line 4

The Experiencer is capable of making a strong stand in the present situation. By staying true to his/her principles, the Experiencer will not make any mistakes.

Line 5

A sudden, unfortunate turn of events has thwarted the Experiencer's progress. There is no blame in this. The Experiencer is advised to accept things as they are and not try to control the flow of events, because this would only lead to a deadlock. If the Experiencer allows events to unfold in their own way, everything will work out for the best.

Line 6

The Experiencer is considering a course of action, but this would be a big mistake. He/she is advised to step back and allow events to unfold in their own way. Over time it will become clear why this particular course of action would have been disastrous. The right way forward will gradually show itself.

26

Biding One's Time

Biding One's Time is almost akin to serving a prison sentence, except there are no jailers. The Experiencer has entered into a situation which had seemed to present a promising future, but instead has only become restrictive and confining. Time drags on and a longing for release from an empty, depressing place weighs heavily on the Experiencer's mind. However, all the doors seem to be closed and simply stepping out is in no way an easy matter. The Experiencer will have to bide his/her time until a way out can be found. In the meantime the Experiencer will have to maintain his/her current position with strength and dignity for as long as it is necessary to do so.

Now is the time to find sources of inspiration and stimulation. The Experiencer has the power and the strength to nourish whatever is deserving of love and care. This task will require commitment and perseverance, day after day. It will ensure that what is precious in the Experiencer's life will not be lost. Any sources of inspiration should be explored that can open a window into the future and reinvigorate the Experiencer with a real sense of purpose. This is the only way to overcome a difficult period of limbo and go on to find release.

Guided by a clear vision of the future the Experiencer will eventually be able to spread his/her wings and leave the prison

---

of restrictive circumstances behind.

The moving lines

Line 1

The Experiencer is not in a position to take any major initiatives during this time. He/she will have to be patient and find a way to cope with a difficult and frustrating situation. Any attempt to make a breakthrough under these circumstances could lead the Experiencer into a serious conflict with others. Therefore the Experiencer is advised to move very cautiously and refrain from becoming too heavily involved in the situation.

Line 2

The Experiencer is prevented from making any real progress. The situation is dominated by unreasonable people who are incapable of making any compromises. Nevertheless, the Experiencer will have the strength to maintain his/her current position for as long as necessary. Eventually the Experiencer will decide to follow an independent path and break free from this restrictive situation.

Line 3

The situation will become untenable. The Experiencer is strongly advised to find a way to get out. This will not be easy. The Experiencer should be fully aware of the risks involved and be prepared to defend his/her interests. Strength and perseverance will be needed to make the necessary transition.

Line 4

As a result of good foresight the Experiencer will be able to counter any negative developments at an early stage. He/she is more than capable of stopping anyone from trying to undermine his/her position. The Experiencer's timely action will prevent any further escalation of the situation.

Line 5
Through diplomacy and clever tactics the Experiencer will be able to prevent a serious abuse of power. Instead of making the mistake of taking powerful people head on, the Experiencer will find a subtle, but effective way to deal with the root of the problem. In this way he/she will be able to limit their power to do harm.

Line 6
The Experiencer has the strength and the awareness to follow the path of destiny. He/she has the inner resources to persevere through the difficulties and eventually find fulfillment.

27

Seeking Nourishment

This hexagram represents the search for societal nourishment, most likely in the form of employment, housing or a business opportunity.

Seeking Nourishment heralds a period in which the Experiencer will have to be very wary. There is a risk of becoming involved with the wrong kind of people and being drawn into a pointless experience that leads absolutely nowhere. During this period the Experiencer's search for nourishment will develop into a learning process in which he/she will become more realistic and less naive.

The Experiencer will need to be very discerning to find the right kind of nourishment. The search for nourishment can lead to encounters with all kinds of people, some of whom are not to be trusted. It is essential to closely observe the people one comes into contact with and try to find out what their real motives and interests are. This is the only way to determine if people are genuine or not, and whether mutual cooperation is truly possible. Success depends on the Experiencer's sound judgment of the people he/she is dealing with.

The Experiencer will have to be very persevering, because the search for nourishment can be a long and sometimes disheartening process.

The search for nourishment often leads to a situation in which the Experiencer discovers that the nourishment he/she desires is not the same as the nourishment he/she really needs. The final outcome may not be spectacular, but it will satisfy the Experiencer's most urgent needs.

The moving lines

Line 1
The Experiencer is considering leaving the present situation. This would be a serious mistake. He/she is advised to remain in the relative security and safety of the current circumstances. The Experiencer should be grateful for his/her good fortune and, for the time being, not look for nourishment elsewhere.

Line 2
The Experiencer is trying to find nourishment, but is straying off the path and looking in the wrong place. By continuing in this way the Experiencer will run the risk of finding nourishment that is only second best and lose sight of the nourishment he/she really needs. This will lead to misfortune.

Line 3
The Experiencer is becoming involved in an activity which will not provide the right kind of nourishment, because it is not in accordance with his/her true nature. The Experiencer is strongly advised not to persevere in this, but to concentrate on finding a way of life that is genuine and meaningful.

Line 4
The Experiencer is looking for the kind of nourishment that nourishes his/her whole being. He/she has the strength and the determination to find out what is truly worthwhile and what is not. In this way the Experiencer will not make any mistakes.

Line 5

The Experiencer is considering a wrong course of action and will not succeed in finding nourishment this way. This is not the right time to make a major transition. The Experiencer should stay in the present situation, because it still offers possibilities for further development.

Line 6

The Experiencer has come to the end of a cycle in his/her life and the present situation no longer provides any nourishment. It is crucial to realize that the current situation will only go downhill and eventually become unsustainable. The time has come to make a major transition. This will succeed and lead to a new beginning.

28

Carrying a Heavy Burden
In this hexagram the I Ching uses the image of a house with a sagging ridge beam; it is close to breaking point.

The Experiencer is under considerable pressure and cannot see the way forward. He/she is trapped and isolated in an increasingly oppressive situation in which there is no future. The Experiencer has reached the absolute limit of what can be achieved in this place, but is nevertheless still emotionally involved in an ongoing effort to make progress under impossible circumstances. In reality nothing can be done to change anything for the better, and any attempts to do so will only be a waste of time and energy.

It is becoming urgent to make an all-out effort to find a way out of this predicament. The Experiencer is carrying an impossibly heavy burden and the stress is starting to take its toll. It would be foolish to continue in this way, because the situation could eventually become very harmful, depleting the Experiencer's physical and mental energy. Breaking free from this bind is the only way forward, but it will involve making some tough decisions. The time has come to let go of any emotional involvement in the situation and move on. The Experiencer has the strength to stand alone and follow an independent path.

The moving lines

Line 1

Only careful and detailed preparation can ensure a successful undertaking at this time. The Experiencer will have to take into account the extent of the opposition he/she will be up against and proceed very cautiously.

Line 2

Although everything appears to have reached a dead end, there is still plenty of life left in the situation. The Experiencer will get new inspiration and discover new ideas which will shape his/her personal growth for years to come.

Line 3

The Experiencer has been trying to persevere in circumstances where progress is no longer possible. A major effort to make progress in the current situation has failed completely and this has left the Experiencer feeling dispirited and exhausted. To prevent any further loss of strength and vitality the Experiencer will have to disengage from the situation and find a way to leave.

Line 4

The Experiencer has succeeded in establishing a secure position in the situation, but should not make the mistake of trying to make any further gains. This would only result in failure. The time has come to start looking for opportunities elsewhere, because the present situation is not going to develop over the longer term.

Line 5

The situation is entering a period of bloom which will be short-lived, because there are no possibilities for any longer term progress. The Experiencer will have to make a transition and find a way of life that can offer a longer term solution.

Line 6

The Experiencer is faced with the task of making a crucial transition. There are many risks involved, but the Experiencer will push on regardless. There is no choice.

The Power of Flowing Water

This hexagram represents the energy of water flowing through a narrow passage. If the water falls into a pit, it will become trapped in a stagnant pool. What is illustrated here is the danger of becoming locked into a negative situation and losing one's power of movement. There is an urgent necessity to build up a momentum and push forward.

The Experiencer has to find a way out of uncertainty, loneliness and isolation, and somehow make a comeback after suffering a serious setback or an exhausting defeat. He/she has no choice but to forge on through the difficulties and the dangers. The alternative is a bleak existence in a totally unsatisfactory situation which will eventually become unsustainable.

The force of flowing water is constant and consistent. Likewise the Experiencer will have to move through these oppressive circumstances with strength and perseverance, acting robustly and decisively whenever necessary. It is crucial to realize that this experience will repeat itself unless a fundamental breakthrough is made, otherwise the Experiencer will only move from one trap into another. The Experiencer's sincerity, consistent and strong, will ensure that he/she will succeed in breaking free.

The moving lines

Line 1
In the midst of many difficulties the Experiencer is pursuing an opportunity to get out of his/her present predicament, but this attempt would only lead the Experiencer into an even more dangerous trap. The Experiencer has completely lost the way and is urged to step back and make a realistic assessment of the serious limitations of the deal on offer.

Line 2
The Experiencer is advised to relax and adapt to the present situation. Any major initiatives at this time would only lead to disappointments and defeat. This is a time to reorientate oneself and develop a new approach to life.

Line 3
The Experiencer should stop trying to take any initiatives in the present situation, because this would only lead to further difficulties. The Experiencer is advised to wait until an opportunity presents itself and then use it as a means to leave the situation.

Line 4
In the midst of many difficulties the Experiencer has the strength to keep going, regardless of any setbacks or disappointments. The Experiencer will be offered a modest opportunity which will help to sustain him/her during this challenging period. Accepting this is no mistake.

Line 5
An opportunity will present itself which will enable the Experiencer to get out of his/her predicament. This may not be exactly what the Experiencer had hoped for, but it should

nevertheless be accepted, because it is the only opportunity available to leave the current difficulties behind and make a new start.

Line 6

The Experiencer has become fixed on a plan for making a major breakthrough. He/she is convinced this plan will succeed, but it is actually completely unrealistic. As a result time and energy will be spent on something that leads nowhere. If the Experiencer abandons his/her cherished plan, the way will open for a real solution that will lead to a release from the current predicament.

30

Clarity

This hexagram represents attaining clarity of mind and purpose. Developing a strong and clear resolve is crucial in the present situation. If the Experiencer is confused or uncertain, it will now be possible to gain a clear understanding of the important issues that will have to be dealt with. A powerful insight will have the effect of clearing the mind, opening the way to follow a true and consistent purpose.

Clarity of mind enables the Experiencer to produce innovative ideas and come up with constructive solutions. Hard work and a strong resolve will make it possible for the Experiencer to team up with others in productive activity. Self-awareness and mutual awareness are the principles that bring people together in common activity. Therefore the Experiencer will need to be sensitive and flexible towards others to attract positive support and create success.

Clarity also refers to having the clarity of mind to focus on an area of activity that is truly suitable to engage in. It will need to be something the Experiencer has a real affinity with and is strongly attracted to. The Experiencer will have to be persevering in this search for a suitable activity, but it will succeed, bringing many rewards and achievements.

The moving lines

Line 1

The Experiencer is confused, but is nevertheless trying to make progress. There are several options available, but the Experiencer will need to proceed carefully; the next move could be a big mistake. The Experiencer is advised to concentrate on gaining a clear understanding of the situation and to take the time to carefully study every option. This is the only way to find the right way forward.

Line 2

The Experiencer has reached a clear insight into the situation and it is now possible to find the right way forward. He/she has all the necessary resources to achieve a major breakthrough.

Line 3

This is a period in which the Experiencer will have to come to terms with the ending of a phase in his/her life. The Experiencer will need to make a major effort to let go of the past and start focusing on the future; otherwise he/she will miss the opportunity to make a new start.

Line 4

The Experiencer is enthusiastically engaging in something, but this will turn out to be short-lived and prove to be worthless in the end.

Line 5

The Experiencer is trying to cope with feelings of deep regret and disappointment. During this period the Experiencer will reach a profound insight into why things went wrong and where he/she has made mistakes in dealing with others. As a result the Experiencer will adopt a completely different approach towards life.

Line 6

When people in power are not worthy of their positions, they will inevitably engage in unethical practices. The Experiencer's sense of duty compels him/her to confront these people head on, regardless of the consequences. The Experiencer is urged to make a distinction between those who have consciously done wrong and those who have only followed orders.

31

Influence (Attraction)

This hexagram represents a situation in which the Experiencer needs to influence and attract others. This is of great importance now, because it will not be possible to succeed without help and support from influential people. The Experiencer is sociable and articulate and therefore more than capable of having a positive influence on others, but the difficulty lies in finding the right people to connect with.

The Experiencer is advised to carefully reconsider his/her wish list and avoid making the mistake of becoming attracted to people or areas of activity which are not worthwhile or feasible. There is a great risk of attracting the wrong people and becoming drawn into relationships that prove to be worthless. The Experiencer will have to be very discerning to distinguish between the people who are of good intentions and those who are not. On the other side, it is equally important to keep an open mind, because opportunities may be found in unexpected places.

The Experiencer will eventually become attracted to something that is truly worthwhile, but time and patience will be needed to allow it to come to fruition. This will succeed in the end. The Experiencer has the power to attract the right people and make the necessary connections to achieve a major breakthrough.

The moving lines

Line 1
An event has influenced the Experiencer in a very profound way and this is inspiring him/her to work towards making a radical change in life.

Line 2
An event has led the Experiencer into making a premature and badly-conceived move. As a result the Experiencer has lost credibility and is in a weakened position. He/she will have to step back and rethink the situation. When the time is ripe, the Experiencer will be able to come up with a new initiative that will succeed.

Line 3
The Experiencer has become strongly attracted to people who are not worthwhile and have nothing to offer. Engaging with these people would be a waste of time and would lead to nothing.

Line 4
The Experiencer is attracted to an opportunity which could provide possibilities for further development. However, he/she is uncertain about it and has been unable to reach a decision. The Experiencer is urged to focus on this opportunity and turn away from the obstacles which are blocking progress in the present situation.

Line 5
The Experiencer will receive interesting news or information which will have a far-reaching effect over the longer term. This will stimulate a process of inner change and result in a concrete plan for the future.

Line 6

The Experiencer has become too involved in a problematic situation and is trying to convince people with persuasive arguments. This will not make any impression. The Experiencer is advised to give up and retreat from the situation.

32

Duration

Duration means persevering on a course of action over a long period of time. It is the power to stay on track and not become deflected or defeated by obstacles. *Duration* also means strengthening the foundation of one's life through finding a long-lasting solution.

Duration marks a significant point on the Experiencer's path of development. He/she has reached a stage in life when it is becoming urgent to find a solution that can stand the test of time. This will only succeed if the Experiencer is pursuing an aim that corresponds with the true purpose of his/her life. Only a strong sense of purpose can provide the staying power needed to keep on course.

The present situation is coming to an end and the Experiencer will have to make a transition. This will be a slow and difficult process and the Experiencer will need to be very persevering in his/her search for a long-lasting solution. It is essential to keep focused on a specific aim and stay on course, even when radical change threatens to sweep everything away, causing feelings of fear and insecurity. Strength of character will be needed to consistently pursue a long-term goal. No matter how difficult the circumstances may be, the Experiencer's strong sense of purpose and steady perseverance will make it possible to push through any obstacles that are obstructing progress. The Experiencer will eventually succeed in making a transition which will open the way for a new beginning.

The moving lines

Line 1

The Experiencer is being too hasty in trying to achieve a long-term solution. If the Experiencer presses forward with this plan, he/she will become trapped in a situation with no future.

Line 2

The Experiencer has the staying power to continue in the present situation, no matter how limiting or frustrating it might be, until a solution can be found. When a breakthrough finally comes, all regrets will disappear.

Line 3

The desire to leave the situation is overwhelming, but the Experiencer will have to develop the staying power to remain in this situation until he/she can find the right opportunity to leave. It is essential to cultivate the strength of character needed to stay on course and work towards a long-term goal. The Experiencer cannot afford to be thrown off balance by any obstacles or challenges along the way.

Line 4

The Experiencer is searching for opportunities, but there are none to be found. This is because the Experiencer is looking for opportunities in the wrong place. Staying power achieves nothing, if one's energy is focused on the unobtainable.

Line 5

The Experiencer has the power to endure, but it would be a

mistake to try to continue in this situation, because it will eventually become unsustainable. The Experiencer is advised to follow an independent path and find a way to leave the situation.

Line 6
The Experiencer is restless and no longer has the heart to remain involved in an activity that is becoming increasingly meaningless. It will not be possible to develop the staying power to persevere with anything until the Experiencer has found the deeper purpose of his/her life.

Retreat

Hexagram *Retreat* ushers in a time when it is absolutely necessary to withdraw from the company of negative people.

There are two different scenarios in this hexagram.

The best-case scenario is a situation in which the Experiencer succeeds in keeping petty people at a distance by displaying a total lack of interest in them, while at the same time vigorously pursuing his/her personal projects or activities. By establishing his/her total independence the Experiencer will completely negate those who desire to dominate the situation.

In the worst-case scenario the Experiencer's efforts to make progress are being completely frustrated by petty, hostile people who are dominating the situation. It would be a serious mistake to try to reach a compromise with these people, which would only be seen as a sign of weakness and encourage them to press home their advantage. It would also be a mistake to pursue any ambitions under these circumstances, because nothing of significance can be accomplished when mediocre people have the upper hand. Trying to make any gains or achieve anything of substance in this situation would be pointless; the Experiencer simply cannot win.

In this scenario the only realistic course of action is to develop an effective exit strategy and leave the situation altogether. In the meantime the Experiencer will need to defend his/her position with strength and dignity until it is possible to make a retreat. It is essential to maintain a correct stand and refuse to be drawn into petty face-to-face hate games. The Experiencer's impeccable behavior and firm attitude will keep his/her enemies at a distance.

Above all else the Experiencer should not see this experience as a defeat. He/she can succeed in maintaining his/her integrity by making a timely and well-organized exit.

The moving lines

Line 1

It is too late to try to leave the situation and, as a result, the Experiencer is completely trapped. Any move now would be very risky and possibly disastrous. The Experiencer will have to adapt to the present circumstances and try to cooperate with the other players in the situation.

Line 2

Bound by duty, the Experiencer is prevented from leaving the situation. He/she can only let go of unnecessary involvement and withdraw as much as possible. In this way the Experiencer will be able to keep unpleasant people at a distance.

Line 3

The Experiencer is trapped in an unpleasant and stressful situation. He/she does not have the power to leave at this time and will have to hold his/her ground. The Experiencer is advised to get help from the other players in the situation to overcome the current difficulties.

Line 4

The Experiencer has an influential and responsible position, but the situation is gradually deteriorating. To avoid making unacceptable compromises the Experiencer will choose to resign his/her position and retreat. The mediocre people in this situation will soon come into difficulties, because they will no longer benefit from the Experiencer's support and guidance.

Line 5

The Experiencer has decided to leave a situation in which progress is blocked by mediocre people. He/she will be able to leave on amicable terms, but is warned to keep to his/her decision and not be tempted into staying.

Line 6

The Experiencer should have no doubts; he/she has found a perfect way to leave unhappy circumstances behind and travel to a new destination.

34

Exercising Restraint

This hexagram represents the power to take strong action, but emphasizes the importance of self-restraint, because it is essential not to act impulsively.

The Experiencer is poised to act. His/her enthusiasm and strong intent produce great powers of persistence and vigor. It is precisely at this point that the Experiencer will need to exercise restraint, step back, and take time for reflection. There may be an attractive opportunity on offer, but it is very important to hold back and not be too easily tempted; a premature move would be a mistake and could lead to missing out on a much better opportunity. Whatever the Experiencer is planning, it will require more thought, and above all else, it must be the right thing to do. The next move must be completely realistic and truly in tune with the Experiencer's path of development.

The Experiencer has the integrity to make perfectly ethical decisions and follow them through. In this case he/she will need to persevere in doing something that is absolutely right. When the time is ripe and everything is properly in place, the Experiencer will be able to act decisively and correctly.

The moving lines

Line 1

The Experiencer has a lot of energy and enthusiasm, but any attempt to force progress at this time will only lead to failure. The Experiencer will need to put more thought into finding ways to make lasting progress.

Line 2

The Experiencer has the energy and the power to achieve a specific aim, but cannot afford to deviate or become overambitious. If the Experiencer is realistic and continues on the present course, it will be possible to enjoy a real achievement.

Line 3

The Experiencer has the energy and the power to press on with an ambitious plan, but is strongly warned not to do so. If the Experiencer perseveres with this plan of action, he/she will become entangled in a hopeless situation which will lead to a major loss of power.

Line 4

The Experiencer has the energy and the power to make great progress during this time. Opportunities are opening up, obstacles will disappear, and the way forward will become clear.

Line 5

The Experiencer has a lot of energy and enthusiasm, but realizes that in the current situation a breakthrough can only be achieved through tact and diplomacy.

Line 6

The Experiencer has a lot of energy and enthusiasm, but is completely stuck in the present situation. When the Experiencer realizes why no further progress is possible, he/she will be able to follow a completely new direction. The Experiencer has the resources to succeed in making a major transition.

Progress

In this hexagram the I Ching uses the image of a brilliant sunrise gradually illuminating the landscape. A new dawn is bringing the promise of significant progress.

This is a time when inner progress begins to gather pace. The mind is open to receive impressions and stimuli from the outer world and a psychological leap forward can be made. Once the Experiencer has reached an insight into the true nature of his/her present circumstances, progress will become possible in a big way.

In an effort to make progress the Experiencer has come up against obstacle after obstacle. A series of unrealistic plans have ended in disappointment and failure. When the Experiencer realizes he/she has been trying to achieve the impossible, the realm of the possible suddenly opens up. A penetrating insight into the current situation enables the Experiencer to give up on any false hopes and recognize the necessity to focus on finding a new direction. This insight will make it possible to draw far-reaching conclusions and make a leap forward. It will be a life-changing experience.

As a result the Experiencer will be able to develop new ideas and a clearer sense of purpose. With renewed self-confidence and optimism the Experiencer will succeed in making important contacts with people, who can offer constructive solutions. This will open the way for major progress.

The moving lines

Line 1
The Experiencer's attempt to make progress is being hampered by a lack of cooperation from others. This is a stressful experience, but the Experiencer will have to accept that it is not possible to win other people's trust under the present circumstances. In the end the Experiencer will come to the conclusion that the situation is hopeless and decide to go his/her own way.

Line 2
The Experiencer is trying to make progress, but will have to cope with a lot of disappointments along the way. Fortunately, the Experiencer has the intuitive power to eventually discover a completely new approach. With perseverance it will be possible to find a way out of the current difficulties and make a new start in a different location.

Line 3
The Experiencer can now make significant progress, but will have to be prepared to take risks. He/she is in a position to make a major transition and will receive the necessary support to do so.

Line 4
The Experiencer is making a mistake by trying to make material gains in the present situation. He/she is strongly advised to stop with this effort and come to terms with the reality. Real progress is no longer possible in the current situation and the time has come to start looking for the way out.

35

Line 5

The Experiencer should be prepared to make the necessary material sacrifices to get out of the present standstill. A major transition is the only way to make progress. This will succeed.

Line 6

The Experiencer is trying to force a breakthrough in an area where progress is no longer possible. Persevering in this would lead to failure. When the Experiencer realizes his/her mistake, another way to make progress will open up. This will succeed.

36

The Darkening of the Light

The Darkening of the Light describes a time when positions of authority are occupied by mediocre or even wicked people, for whom maintaining their own positions is far more important than serving the general good.

The Experiencer is at risk of becoming a target for vindictive people and will need to keep a low profile to avoid drawing their attention. The light of the Experiencer cannot shine in these circumstances; he/she will have to live in obscurity, receiving little or no recognition from anyone in society. Oppressed by extremely adverse conditions, the Experiencer is forced to remain hidden, carrying out his/her daily activities in complete anonymity with the quiet hope that better times will come.

Above all else, the Experiencer must keep the inner light burning, otherwise the darkness of the times will extinguish whatever hope and optimism remain. In the time of *The Darkening of the Light* the future is obscured and the challenge is to find a way through the darkness by shedding light on the future and working towards it step by step. The first step forward will be to gain an understanding of the underlying meaning of these difficult circumstances. The Experiencer will learn about the twisted nature of wicked people by observing the devious ways in which they seek to dominate and manipulate others. It will then be possible to develop an effective strategy to cope with the intimidating behavior of these people. The next step will be to find a way out of this oppressive situation. With optimism and strength the Experiencer will eventually succeed in breaking free.

The moving lines

Line 1
The burden of living amongst unpleasant people in extremely oppressive circumstances is very heavy indeed. The situation has actually become untenable and the only option open to the Experiencer is to leave. He/she does not have the power to make a major transition, but will receive enough support to get out of the situation. Nevertheless, the Experiencer will become the victim of malicious gossip.

Line 2
The Experiencer is isolated and living in complete obscurity. He/she has been unable to get any recognition whatsoever. Furthermore, he/she is experiencing a severe setback which is only making things worse. The time has come to find a way to move on. Fortunately, the Experiencer has the power to make a major transition into much better circumstances.

Line 3
The Experiencer has the power to confront wrongdoers in an oppressive situation, but lacks the power to force through any major reforms. The Experiencer will have to withdraw and find a new direction in life.

Line 4
The Experiencer has become fully aware of the plans and motives of his/her enemies and realizes he/she will not have the

power to counteract. The Experiencer will have to flee from the situation and get out of danger before it is too late.

Line 5
The Experiencer is fully aware that no further development is possible under the present circumstances; the situation has peaked and is now in decline. The Experiencer is working on a plan to get out, but this will take time. In the meantime it is essential to keep a low profile and be diplomatic, because the Experiencer's position is weak and vulnerable.

Line 6
In pursuit of an ambitious undertaking the Experiencer is confronted with forces he/she has no power to counteract. The Experiencer is losing his/her position of influence and will have to give up on any ambitions in this situation. This will usher in a period of reflection which will provide an opportunity to discover a more genuine and authentic way of life.

The Home

The Home represents a dwelling, a place of abode where companions live together in a mutually supportive relationship. A caring home environment is of great importance, because it provides a situation where people can make a stand in the world and endure together. Therefore *The Home* is also a place of retreat, where companions can withdraw from the difficulties of the outer world and find solace in one another.

However, this hexagram is not about living in isolation. It refers to an ongoing experience of intelligently and carefully relating to events and developments in the outer world. This is very important, because the current situation has reached a stage of development that is becoming too static and limiting. Further development will require new initiatives and perhaps a venture into a completely different area. To influence and convince others the Experiencer will need to be consistent and clear in his/her words and actions.

The Home can also represent the need to withdraw and completely reconsider one's aims and plans. This is particularly necessary when an initiative has come to nothing and one is forced to find a new direction. Fortunately, the Experiencer has the possibility to withdraw into a pleasant and supportive home environment and take time to consider various options for the future.

The moving lines

Line 1
The Experiencer enjoys a harmonious home life. This provides a strong base from which to gradually work towards a goal and make societal progress. Therefore the Experiencer is advised to continue in the current situation and avoid making any drastic decisions at this time.

Line 2
The Experiencer has very little power or influence and cannot achieve any ambitions at this time. He/she should simply concentrate on maintaining his/her household and find happiness in the little joys of everyday life. The Experiencer's harmonious home life will provide stability and strength during this difficult period.

Line 3
The Experiencer is going through a stressful period and this is having a negative impact on his/her home life. The stress is caused by a lack of direction and clear purpose. It is important to discuss this problem within the home and try to find the right way forward.

Line 4
The Experiencer's reliability and sense of responsibility has made a very positive impression on other people. He/she is enjoying their trust and a situation of mutual cooperation is developing. As a result the Experiencer will be able to maintain a strong base and enjoy a very harmonious home life.

Line 5
The Experiencer enjoys a harmonious home life. This is very fortunate, because it enables the Experiencer to follow an

authentic path and develop his/her inner resources during a time when it is very difficult to make societal progress.

Line 6

The Experiencer has reached the peak of his/her development in this situation. Fortunately, he/she has built up an excellent reputation and is widely respected and trusted. This will enable the Experiencer to make a successful transition when it becomes necessary to do so.

38

Discord

Discord represents a situation in which the Experiencer is at odds with others and there is a real risk of becoming involved in a serious conflict. The problem is that the Experiencer is in the wrong place at the wrong time, but it is not easy to overcome this dilemma.

The Experiencer is living in a place where it is difficult to establish positive relations with other people. They tend to be narrow-minded and clannish, and the Experiencer has very little affinity with them. He/she has a completely different outlook on life and this is leading to a clash of opposites. The Experiencer is increasingly seen as an outsider and an upstart, particularly when he/she dares to complain about any wrongdoings in the community. Furthermore, there is a definite sense of impending decline in the situation; people are changeable, unpredictable, and often preoccupied with trivial or childish pursuits. The Experiencer will need to keep a distance from the various groups or cliques who are established in this place.

There are several possible scenarios in the time of *Discord* and in each one the Experiencer is up against real problems with people. In the best-case scenario *Discord* is overcome by attracting strong allies and establishing a position of strength that no one can challenge. Alternatively, the Experiencer succeeds in breaking free from the situation by attracting help from sympathetic people. The most difficult scenario is a confrontation with someone who has abused his/her position of power; in this case the Experiencer will succeed in defeating a powerful opponent.

Discord will challenge the Experiencer to stand alone and be completely independent. The Experiencer has the strength to grapple with a difficult fate and follow his/her destiny.

The moving lines

Line 1
From a position of almost complete isolation the Experiencer engages in a vigorous effort to make societal progress. However, the situation fails to yield any opportunities and the entire effort grinds to a halt. Deprived of the power to act decisively the Experiencer is left trying to cope with feelings of impotence and regret. An increasing sense of desperation could put the Experiencer at risk of making a serious mistake. It is therefore of paramount importance to be on guard against people with bad intentions. In due time the way forward will start to open up and the Experiencer will be able to act again.

Line 2
The Experiencer is in an isolated position and progress is painfully slow. He/she is becoming increasingly concerned about the direction his/her life is taking. Suddenly, an unexpected event triggers a crucial insight and the Experiencer sees the direction he/she will have to follow. This is the path of destiny.

Line 3
The Experiencer pushes forward in an effort to make progress, but strong opposition causes the Experiencer's initiative to end

in a humiliating failure. The Experiencer is forced to step back and wait for a better opportunity to realize his/her plan.

Line 4

The Experiencer is trying to cope with a conflict situation without any support from anybody. He/she is running the risk of a damaging confrontation with unpleasant people. Fortunately, the Experiencer will succeed in finding allies and with their help achieve an important aim without making any mistakes.

Line 5

The Experiencer is in an isolated position, but will nevertheless succeed in getting help to achieve a much-needed breakthrough. He/she will have to be open-minded and welcome any potential allies who can offer support. This will enable the Experiencer to make a major transition and follow the path of destiny.

Line 6

The Experiencer is in an unpleasant situation amongst nasty, mediocre people with little prospect of improvement. An unexpected change will occur which the Experiencer at first will view with distrust. Eventually, he/she will come to see this event as a blessing in disguise, because it provides a timely opportunity to get out of a hopeless situation.

39

Obstruction

The Experiencer is following a wrong course of action and is coming up against an obstacle that cannot be overcome. The time has come to let go of a cherished idea or dream that is impossible to achieve. If the Experiencer keeps trying to achieve the impossible, he/she will only become locked in a futile effort to make progress. The solution is to turn away from the obstacle and give up trying, however painful this may be. When the Experiencer lets go, he/she will be released from an all-consuming effort and be able to look at the situation with fresh eyes.

Finding another way to make progress will be a slow and difficult process. The Experiencer will have to develop a completely different approach to overcome the problems he/she is facing. It is essential to take the time to carefully consider any options available. Patience and self-honesty will be needed to make a realistic assessment of what is possible and what is not. The Experiencer might have to settle for a humble solution, because the time has come to find a way out of isolation, doing whatever it takes. The only way to get back into the stream of life is to connect with people who can be of real assistance. By adopting a realistic plan and following it through until the end the Experiencer will succeed in making a new beginning.

The moving lines

Line 1

If the Experiencer pushes forward now, he/she will come up against an obstacle that cannot be overcome. The Experiencer is advised to step back and allow the situation to develop until the way forward becomes clear.

Line 2

In an effort to make societal progress the Experiencer meets with obstacle after obstacle. This is not the Experiencer's fault; there are simply no opportunities available. The Experiencer will need to consider moving to a different location to make progress.

Line 3

The Experiencer's plan to make progress is bound to fail because insurmountable obstacles are blocking the way. Fortunately, the Experiencer will see this in time and abandon his/her plan. In this way he/she will avoid wasting time and resources on a pursuit that would have led nowhere.

Line 4

The Experiencer's efforts to make progress will only run into obstacles that cannot be overcome. By stepping back and trying a different approach the Experiencer will succeed in connecting up with the right people.

Line 5

The Experiencer is in a very difficult situation. All efforts to make progress have failed. The Experiencer is advised to stop trying to overcome the obstacles alone, because help will eventually come from unexpected quarters.

Line 6

The Experiencer should stay on course and keep following a specific aim, because in this way it will be possible to work towards a longer term goal. Any deviation from this path will only lead into obstacles and difficulties.

40

Deliverance

Deliverance represents a sudden and powerful movement to get out of danger, out of a trap. It is the release from a situation in which there is no longer any future. This does not happen easily.

The Experiencer is struggling to cope with a deeply disappointing experience that has led absolutely nowhere. All hopes and aspirations have come to nothing, leaving a bitter taste of failure and defeat. Trapped in an increasingly hopeless situation, the Experiencer feels an overwhelming desire to break free, and starts searching for a way out. However, it soon becomes clear that there are very few possibilities for making a breakthrough. The only way forward is to follow the path of least resistance by taking the obvious and most realistic way out. The Experiencer will then succeed in breaking free.

The liberation from oppressive and confining circumstances is euphoric, releasing pent-up energy and dispelling the gloom of sorrow. The Experiencer can now make a break with the past, and find it in his/her heart to forgive any wrongdoers and let go of all regrets. In this way he/she will experience renewal and regain the optimism needed to make a fresh start.

Events move very quickly in the time of *Deliverance* and the exhilarating experience of release is soon over. When the Experiencer arrives at his/her destination, new challenges and opportunities will present themselves. It will then be extremely important to keep an open mind, because the Experiencer is entering unknown territory. A cautious and diplomatic approach will be essential to secure and maintain a safe position.

The moving lines

Line 1

It is not worthwhile trying to stop the ongoing decline in the present situation. Everything is gradually coming to an end and this is simply inevitable. The breakup of the situation will release the Experiencer to start a new phase in his/her life.

Line 2

With strength and perseverance the Experiencer will be able to deal successfully with problems that have arisen in the situation. As a result the Experiencer can continue on the present course of action with confidence and enthusiasm.

Line 3

The Experiencer is carrying a burden of responsibility that is too heavy to bear. Persevering with this would lead to serious difficulties and failure. The Experiencer will need to let go of this burden and find a new direction in life.

Line 4

The Experiencer's efforts to find a way out of a discouraging situation, in which there are no opportunities, have been without success. He/she is advised to stop trying and let things develop on their own. In due course an effective solution will present itself that will enable the Experiencer to move on from this situation.

Line 5

The Experiencer has become entangled in an oppressive situation that is dominated by mediocre people. With strength and perseverance he/she will nevertheless be able to break free from this difficult predicament. When it becomes clear that the Experiencer is determined to leave the situation, nobody will try to prevent this.

Line 6

The Experiencer can now deal successfully with a major problem that is presenting a serious obstacle to progress. This will set the Experiencer free to make a major transition.

Decrease

Decrease is a time of grief and severe limitations. There is a deep feeling of loss and failure.

As a result of a serious setback the Experiencer is forced to live in greatly reduced circumstances. He/she is struggling to cope with a series of unfortunate events that have led to a dead-end situation with many restrictions and very little freedom. The feeling of disillusionment and futility is almost overwhelming, leaving the Experiencer drained of energy and vitality.

Patience and restraint are needed now to cope with a disappointing and frustrating situation in which one has very little power to act. An important step forward is to try to accept things as they are, because it is not possible to change anything in the present circumstances. With sincerity and strength the Experiencer will be able to maintain his/her current position and eventually find a way to make progress, regardless of the difficulties.

In the time to come the Experiencer should search for a new direction and develop a new purpose for the future. The Experiencer cannot afford to lose heart and should continue to believe in his/her ability to overcome failure and find success. The Experiencer should take encouragement from reviewing his/her past accomplishments and be confident that, when the opportunity arises, his/her talents can be put to use again.

The time of *Decrease* will inevitably come to an end and an opportunity will present itself to make a fresh start.

The moving lines

Line 1
It is becoming urgent to team up with other people and reach an agreement to work on a shared purpose. This would greatly benefit all parties concerned. When this task is accomplished, the Experiencer will be free to move on.

Line 2
It would be a mistake to look for opportunities elsewhere; this would only lead to misfortune. The Experiencer should continue in the present situation, because there is more to be accomplished. Perseverance will create success for the Experiencer and this will also benefit others.

Line 3
The Experiencer will have to accept that he/she will remain isolated in the present situation. Trying to link up with an existing group would lead to failure, because the Experiencer will not be accepted as a member of the group. When the Experiencer follows an independent path, he/she will eventually find companions.

Line 4
It is essential for the Experiencer to overcome feelings of anxiety and make an effort to change his/her attitude. It will then become possible to attract other people's sympathy and support and succeed in getting out of isolation.

Line 5

The Experiencer will receive a good deal of support to accomplish an important task. Nobody will be able to oppose this. As a result of this achievement the Experiencer will win the trust and respect of the other players in the situation.

Line 6

The Experiencer has the opportunity to accomplish an important task for the common good. Strength and perseverance will be needed, but plenty of help and support will be available. When the Experiencer has completed this task, it will be crucial to step back and stop trying to achieve more, because there is a limit to what can be accomplished in the situation.

42

Increase

This hexagram represents a time when personal growth is the only way to develop out of a static situation and eventually make a major transition. The Experiencer has the energy to embark on something new, but will need to gain the necessary insight to do so.

Increase ushers in a time of growing maturity and strength of character. Day by day, in the midst of difficult circumstances, a slow and profound process of personal development is taking place. The Experiencer is learning lessons from past mistakes, becoming increasingly aware of how his/her hopes and aspirations have shaped and determined everything that has happened until now. This will make it possible to come to terms with the past and accept the present reality.

The Experiencer will see the futility of trying to make a lasting success in a situation where selfish people have the upper hand. But nothing has been lost. The Experiencer's energy is stronger than ever and his/her deepest aspirations are still alive and intact. New insights and a more mature attitude will make it possible to overcome the present difficulties and make a major transition. By taking full responsibility for choices made in the past the Experiencer will become the creator of a new life.

The moving lines

Line 1

The Experiencer is engaging in an important project, a work of great significance, which will be of considerable benefit to others. This work will require tremendous energy and perseverance, but in the end it will be a deeply fulfilling experience.

Line 2

The Experiencer is working on an important project. Fortunately, he/she will receive a great deal of support and as a result nobody will be able to oppose it. With strength and perseverance the Experiencer will be able to achieve a lasting solution which will receive the seal of approval from people in authority.

Line 3

The Experiencer will gain in wisdom by living through times of adversity. By being sincere in everything he/she does the Experiencer will be able to have an important influence on others.

Line 4

It is essential to be diplomatic and correct. Keeping people in authority properly informed will ensure their support. As a result the Experiencer will succeed in relocating to a better place. A new location will provide the perfect setting for the Experiencer to engage in an ongoing creative success.

Line 5

The Experiencer will achieve something of worth that will not only benefit him/herself, but will also benefit others. This will create a lot of goodwill. As a result the Experiencer will receive all the nourishment he/she needs. There is no need to have any doubt about this.

Line 6

The Experiencer is confused and becoming too self-centered. As a result he/she is dangerously out of tune with the situation and is pushing things too hard. This will have dire consequences; the Experiencer will be on the receiving end of a nasty attack. The only solution will be to seek help and try to reach a compromise. In this way it will be possible to make a fresh start.

43

Breakthrough

This hexagram represents the necessity to take decisive action to achieve a breakthrough. However, this action will need to be carefully planned; only the right action at the right time will achieve the much desired breakthrough.

The Experiencer is entangled in a situation where wicked and corrupt people have the upper hand. Progress is impossible in these circumstances; the Experiencer's antagonists are succeeding in making his/her position almost untenable. The temptation to confront these wrongdoers face to face is great, but any attempts to score a victory in this way would be disastrous. The Experiencer should at all costs avoid an open confrontation with these people, because this would only lead to serious trouble and conflict.

Instead of trying to deal with the problems alone, the Experiencer should go to people in authority for help and inform them of the seriousness of the situation. By pointing out who the wrongdoers are and revealing the extent of their corrupt activities, the Experiencer will succeed in getting a certain amount of support and assistance. However, the authorities have only limited powers to act in this situation, but some action will be taken to curb the activities of these wrongdoers, giving the Experiencer a much-needed respite from a nasty struggle.

Unfortunately, this will be a hollow victory. The Experiencer has made some formidable enemies and the situation remains deadlocked. Nevertheless, the Experiencer's decisive action has created a window of opportunity to find a way out of this predicament. If the Experiencer grabs this opportunity and is willing to make the necessary material sacrifices, he/she will be able to break free.

The moving lines

Line 1
The desire to make a breakthrough is very strong, but any premature moves would be disastrous. The Experiencer's current plans are ill-conceived and will certainly lead to failure. It is crucial to hold back and take the time to work on a realistic plan of action.

Line 2
A drastic change is on the way. However, the Experiencer should have no doubts or anxieties, because he/she is fully capable of taking the necessary measures to make a major transition.

Line 3
The Experiencer has embarked on a resolute course of action, but is encountering serious difficulties. The Experiencer is acting alone without any support from others and as a result is coming under criticism. Nevertheless, following an independent course is not a mistake.

Line 4
The Experiencer has been too headstrong in trying to make a breakthrough. Single-mindedly pursuing an unrealistic goal has led nowhere. The Experiencer is urged to let go of his/her cherished ideas and let events take their course. A possibility

for a breakthrough will present itself in an unexpected way.

Line 5

The time has come to make a major breakthrough. The Experiencer will need considerable determination to push through the difficulties on his/her path, but it is the only way to get out of a worthless situation. This will succeed.

Line 6

The Experiencer cannot afford to be complacent or indulge in wishful thinking. The current situation will seriously deteriorate, if the Experiencer fails to take action. It is crucial to act before it is too late; missing the window of opportunity for a breakthrough will lead to misfortune in the end.

44

Encounters

This hexagram represents a time of encounters with deceptive people whose selfish motives are concealed behind a facade of good intentions. These encounters begin well in an atmosphere of friendship and trust and then take a turn for the worse. This is a completely unexpected, often shocking experience.

The Experiencer is advised to be extremely cautious in all dealings with other people. There is a great risk of becoming involved with people who are absolutely not worthwhile. It is especially important to resist any tempting offers, which could lead to disappointment, or even conflict. Although the desire to link up with others is very great at this time, the Experiencer should be very careful and avoid engaging with the wrong kind of people. During the time of *Encounters* the Experiencer is at serious risk of mingling with people who seek to have power over the Experiencer's life, with the sole intention to belittle and to dominate. Such encounters could develop into a situation in which the Experiencer is forced to withdraw from people behaving in an unpleasant and unreasonable way in order to avoid a nasty, drawn-out conflict.

In the worst-case scenario the Experiencer needs the courage to confront stubborn and devious people head on, point out their shortcomings, and sever relations with them. The Experiencer has the strength and the resources to continue on his/her journey alone, regardless of setbacks.

The moving lines

Line 1
The Experiencer is strongly advised to stop running around in search of opportunities. Continuing in this way will lead to encounters with the wrong kind of people, which will end in misfortune. He/she should persevere in the present situation, because it will provide a real opportunity for future development.

Line 2
The Experiencer has something precious and unique, but should not try to share it with people who are not worthwhile. It is better to withdraw and stay alone than seek out the company of the wrong kind of people.

Line 3
The Experiencer is meeting with serious opposition and progress has become extremely difficult. If the Experiencer is aware of the danger of conflict, he/she will be able to avoid making serious mistakes.

Line 4
The Experiencer is very isolated and has been unable to link up with other people. In such a situation there is a great risk of attracting the antagonism of petty, small-minded people by making the wrong move. The Experiencer is strongly advised to find a way out of this predicament by linking up with people who are worthwhile.

Line 5

The Experiencer has special personal qualities, but is isolated, because there are no opportunities available to share his/her talents with others. The Experiencer's situation is nevertheless beneficial, because it provides the perfect setting for significant personal development.

Line 6

The Experiencer has been making a robust effort to get out of isolation, but has been unable to find worthwhile people to link up with. Realizing that this effort is leading nowhere, the Experiencer stops trying and decides to follow an independent path.

45

Gathering Together

Gathering Together represents a community or a workplace, where people are gathered together to live or work. The success or failure of such a community is dependent on the mutual cooperation of the people and the quality and stature of the leadership.

The Experiencer is living or working in a community that is suffering from an ongoing failure of leadership and a lack of cooperation between people. This is a situation in which the Experiencer will have to be on guard and be prepared for any unforeseen developments. Where birds of a feather gather together, the unpleasant tendencies of undesirable people will become manifest. For this reason it is very important to build good relations with any strong and socially active members of the community. Strong allies could prove to be indispensable, because there is a real possibility the Experiencer will have to counter negative or provocative behavior during this period. The challenge under these circumstances is to follow a strong purpose, focus on specific aims and gradually work towards achieving them. Over time the Experiencer's moral and spiritual discipline will ensure his/her success in winning through a complex and difficult situation.

Gathering Together can also refer to a scenario in which the

Experiencer is living in isolation in a community as an outsider. Nevertheless, when the opportunity arises to make a contribution to the community, the Experiencer should welcome it, because he/she has the ability to accomplish something that is of real worth.

The moving lines

Line 1
The Experiencer is anxious and confused. Sometimes things go well, but difficulties keep coming up. He/she is wondering if it is really worthwhile making a long-term commitment to stay in the current situation. The Experiencer is urged to focus on a deeper purpose in life; this is the only way to overcome confusion. He/she should not hesitate to leave the situation and follow the path of destiny.

Line 2
The Experiencer is looking for an opportunity to link up with others and step out of isolation. An unexpected opportunity to link up with the right people will present itself. The Experiencer should not hesitate to grasp this opportunity, because it will lead to good fortune. The Experiencer's sincerity and moral strength will meet with recognition at last.

Line 3
The Experiencer is in a situation fraught with difficulties and disagreements. The only way forward is to try to get support and assistance from people who have the power to provide concrete help.

Line 4
The Experiencer is prepared to withdraw from making a deal with the wrong people. In this way a serious mistake can be

avoided. The Experiencer will have to press on until a genuine opportunity presents itself.

Line 5

The Experiencer has succeeded in linking up with others, but has no power to influence the situation. Having a position without influence will only lead to disillusionment. Eventually the Experiencer will need to move on.

Line 6

The Experiencer's disappointment is completely justified. He/she has achieved a long-desired goal, only to discover that his/her position is very insecure. The Experiencer has no allies in the situation and is not receiving any support. This is not the Experiencer's fault; the situation has reached a standstill and is going into decline.

46

Authentic Development

In this hexagram the I Ching uses the image of a tiny sapling, slowly pushing its way up through the earth. The slow growth of a tree symbolizes the gradual development of the Experiencer's talents and expertise.

Authentic Development means following a higher aim in life through exploring and developing the hidden talents one possesses. This is a time when the Experiencer's special gifts and talents are slowly gaining in strength, opening up a period of growth which will lead to a new cycle in his/her life.

The current situation is only a stepping stone, a place where slow, incremental progress can be made towards a future destination. The Experiencer should not have any expectations of success in the present circumstances; he/she is stranded in a place of little opportunity. A time will come when the Experiencer will need to consider where the future really is.

During this period the Experiencer will be able to explore and develop his/her potential and examine all the things that are of importance in his/her life. Any worthwhile projects or ideas should be treated as valuables and kept safe for the future. All these precious things will eventually be assembled to form the basis for a new life. This process will gradually lead to a point where the Experiencer will be able to develop a clear aim and a plan for the future. A concrete plan will make it possible to start an effective search for new opportunities.

The moving lines

Line 1

The Experiencer has succeeded in winning the trust and confidence of others and as a result is living in very beneficial circumstances. These are the perfect conditions which will enable the Experiencer to go through a period of significant personal development.

Line 2

The Experiencer is strong and persevering in pursuing an important goal. However, this will be a long and difficult journey and the Experiencer will have to maintain his/her strength and integrity in a challenging world, never losing sight of the goal. Eventually, the Experiencer's sincerity and merit will lead to recognition and fulfillment.

Line 3

This is the right time to engage in a systematic effort to find out if one's ideas are feasible. Even if there are no concrete opportunities to be found, this exercise will at least be an important reality check. As a result of this process of elimination the Experiencer will be able to draw conclusions and make realistic plans.

Line 4

This is a situation in which the Experiencer will need to accept the way things are organized. If the Experiencer adapts to the current situation, he/she will be able to engage in important work and make real progress over the longer term.

Line 5

With patience and perseverance it will be possible to make progress, a step at a time. This is the only way the Experiencer will be able to achieve his/her aims.

Line 6

The Experiencer is engaged in a protracted struggle to make progress in a situation which has been spoiled by others. It will be impossible to achieve a total victory in this struggle; trying to do so will only lead to exhaustion. The Experiencer is advised to hold on to the real purpose of his/her life and find a way to move on from this situation.

47

Exhaustion

This hexagram represents the challenge of coping with an adverse fate and somehow finding the strength to overcome it.

The Experiencer is trapped in an oppressive situation and all attempts to make progress have led to nothing. In an all-out search for opportunities or support the Experiencer has only met with a lack of sympathy and interest. All efforts have been in vain, draining the Experiencer's energy and enthusiasm. This has led to exhaustion.

During this period it is very important to use every opportunity to withdraw and rest to replenish lost energy. Any further attempts to try to influence or convince people in this situation would be futile. The people the Experiencer is trying to deal with are small-minded and mediocre, and they certainly do not trust outsiders. The Experiencer will have to rely on his/her inner resources to cope with an unpleasant situation in which he/she is completely marginalized. This is a time to be totally independent, to stand alone and follow a strong purpose, no matter what other people may think.

The Experiencer will emerge from this episode a stronger and more resourceful person, capable of coming to grips with a difficult fate. When the time comes he/she will be ready to strike out and get back into the stream of life, using whatever means possible. Great perseverance and iron determination will be needed to achieve this. In the end the Experiencer will succeed in breaking free from this situation.

The moving lines

Line 1
In the midst of oppressive circumstances the Experiencer has been unable to make any progress. This has led to exhaustion and depression. The time has come to shake off any feelings of apathy and make a major effort to get out. The Experiencer has the ability to break free from this predicament and should be prepared to take risks to regain his/her freedom. The release from this unhappy situation will lead to joy.

Line 2
The Experiencer is living in comfort, but the circumstances are unhappy and oppressive. Nevertheless, it would be premature to try to leave the situation at this time; to do so would only lead to misfortune. An unexpected opportunity will present itself that will give the Experiencer the chance to engage in something truly worthwhile. This opportunity should be grasped; it will enable the Experiencer to make important connections which will have positive implications for the future.

Line 3
The Experiencer's situation has become untenable. He/she is up against formidable obstacles and is not receiving any support. Continuing to live in this way will become unbearable. The Experiencer is strongly advised to take charge of his/her life and start looking for the way out.

Line 4

The Experiencer is clinging to a cherished plan which he/she believes will bring an end to the current difficulties. But pursuing this plan has only led the Experiencer into an extremely oppressive situation. If the Experiencer comes to terms with the reality and abandons his/her plan, the way out of this predicament will open up.

Line 5

The Experiencer has been too robust in a major attempt to make progress and as a result everything has ground to a halt. He/she is advised to carefully and patiently find a way to attract support from others. A way out of the difficulties will then gradually open up. It will be necessary to make material sacrifices to break free from this situation.

Line 6

The Experiencer has become entangled in an exhausting conflict. Any attempts to continue trying to make progress in this situation will lead into serious trouble. The Experiencer is advised to put aside any regrets and find a way to get out of this predicament. The road ahead is difficult, but everything will work out in the end.

48

The Well

In this hexagram the I Ching uses *the well* as a symbol for the source of nourishment. This image represents the outer well and the inner well.

The *outer well* is the communal well, which is the societal source of nourishment. It is a physical location which provides nourishment in the form of social interaction and work opportunities. The Experiencer can only draw the water from the communal well, if he/she can gain access to it.

The *inner well* is the Experiencer's inner source of talents and abilities from which he/she can draw nourishment in the form of energy and purpose. The water of the inner well can only be used effectively if it is clear and clean. Clarity of mind and a clear sense of purpose are essential for the Experiencer's inner source to become an actual resource. If this is the case and the Experiencer has access to a good communal well, he/she will be able to encourage others to work together for the common good.

In the present situation the Experiencer is faced with the problem of finding a good communal well to draw nourishment from. He/she will need to draw from the inner well for inspiration to strengthen his/her energy and sense of purpose. Only when the Experiencer's inner well is in good order, will it be possible to find nourishment from a communal well with any chance of success. If the Experiencer has difficulty finding societal nourishment in his/her current location, it may become necessary to move to a different location and find a better well.

The moving lines

Line 1
The Experiencer is stranded in the wrong location. This is a place people have abandoned, because the communal well is drying up. The Experiencer will not be able to find nourishment here much longer. When an opportunity presents itself, the Experiencer should take it and move on.

Line 2
The Experiencer will not be able to draw any nourishment from this well. The communal well at this location has nothing to offer. The Experiencer is advised to give up on this well and look elsewhere for opportunities.

Line 3
The Experiencer is not getting any recognition, which is unfortunate, because he/she has a lot to offer. The Experiencer will have to look for opportunities elsewhere. Strength and perseverance will be needed in this ongoing search to find recognition, but the Experiencer will succeed in the end.

Line 4
The Experiencer has been learning from past mistakes and is building up his/her inner resources. As a result the Experiencer will be able to follow an independent path and leave the present location to search for a good communal well elsewhere.

Line 5
The Experiencer's inner well is a source of great potential and therefore he/she has a lot to offer. The Experiencer has outgrown the present situation and the time has come to look for new opportunities.

Line 6
The Experiencer has great potential, but must now make every effort to realize this potential in the reality. Fulfillment can only be achieved in the world of activity. If the Experiencer makes the effort to reach out and connect with the right people, it will be possible to make great progress.

The Revolution

This hexagram represents radical change, which begins on a subjective, personal level and eventually extends into the reality.

The Experiencer is faced with the challenge of making a fundamental change in his/her life. The urgency to do so is becoming increasingly apparent; the Experiencer is in a restrictive situation and has been unable to make any significant progress. However, change is in the air and possibilities are presenting themselves which will open the way for the drastic change *The Revolution* represents.

The inner revolution is already underway; it is the Experiencer's reaction to an unfulfilling situation and the growing perception that his/her present lifestyle is leading nowhere. The Experiencer will need to develop a new perspective on life by relinquishing outdated aspects of his/her personality and allowing them to recede into the past. This means letting go of old ideas and dreams in order to find a new direction in life.

A successful revolution requires the foresight to anticipate precisely what kind of change is necessary, together with the self-discipline to carefully plan and, with perfect timing, enact such a move. In this way the Experiencer will succeed in taking the necessary steps to radically change his/her life. When the time is ripe, the Experiencer will see the right way to act and either convince people in authority to help him/her to radically change the current situation or abandon the situation and move on.

The moving lines

Line 1

Stepping out of old habits and routines is not an easy thing to do; nevertheless, the need for change is becoming increasingly urgent. Continuing in the old way will inevitably lead the Experiencer to a dead end. If the Experiencer focuses on the need for radical change, he/she will find new inspiration and attract support from the right people to start a new life.

Line 2

Change is in the air. If the Experiencer proceeds carefully, he/she will be able to achieve a major breakthrough. This cannot be achieved without help. The Experiencer does not have the power to act alone and will therefore have to win the trust and support of others. When everything is in place and the timing is right, it will be possible to take decisive action.

Line 3

Faced with the prospect of having to make a radical change in his/her life, the Experiencer is trying to find a way out of a situation which has reached a dead end. Change is in the air, but cannot be speeded up. The Experiencer is warned not to act prematurely, because the way out is not yet clear and any actions taken now would only lead to failure. The Experiencer is advised to follow developments and wait for the right time to act.

Line 4

The Experiencer will be able to play a crucial role in overturning the status quo, thereby changing the current power structure. This will have the effect of preventing any further decline in the current situation and as a result the Experiencer's circumstances will greatly improve.

Line 5

The Experiencer is going through a profound process of personal change. He/she is seeing things in a new light and as a result is making a critical assessment of the current situation. The Experiencer has the strength and the clarity to make tough decisions and radically change his/her approach to life.

Line 6

The Experiencer has gone through a process of radical personal change. He/she has developed the strength and depth of character that commands respect. As a result the Experiencer will be able to influence other people in the situation and win their cooperation. Nevertheless, trying to force change too quickly would have disastrous results. If the Experiencer is patient and persevering, he/she will be successful in achieving a gradual change for the better.

50

The Cauldron

The Cauldron represents the process of developing self-knowledge and wisdom. The process of inner growth leading to self-realization is likened to cooking food in a cauldron; it is a slow and intensive process in which the individual undergoes a gradual transformation.

The Experiencer has reached a point in life when he/she is faced with the challenge of having to start anew. A radical change in the Experiencer's life has swept away the old, but there is nothing new to replace it. He/she has stepped out of an old lifestyle and entered a situation that will require a completely new approach towards life. The past is vanishing, losing its relevance, and personal change is the only way to move forward.

A difficult, sometimes painful process of soul searching will mark a period of confusion and disorientation. Leaving the old behind creates a situation in which the Experiencer will undergo a gradual transformation until a point is reached when he/she is ready to enter a new phase in life. None of this is easy. The Experiencer will be confronted with the challenge of having to change his/her attitudes and ideas, abandoning cherished dreams that have proven to be worthless. In the end, the Experiencer will emerge with a deeper insight into his/her destiny, having reached a greater understanding of who he/she really is. This personal transformation will enable the Experiencer to embark on a new life.

The moving lines

Line 1

By getting rid of old, entrenched ideas the Experiencer will be able to enter new territory and make significant progress. He/she has the resources to make a new start in life.

Line 2

The Experiencer has developed the potential to make significant achievements and has the resources to do so. Unfortunately, this has attracted the enmity and jealousy of others. Nevertheless, no one will succeed in harming the Experiencer. The present situation has served its purpose and the Experiencer is ready to move on. A major transition is on the cards, but the Experiencer will need to give this very careful consideration.

Line 3

The current situation represents an opportunity to do away with the old and explore new ideas. The Experiencer is urged to put aside ambitions and dreams that belong to the past. Pursuing old ideas in a search for opportunities will only lead the Experiencer into places where his/her talents cannot shine. It is infinitely better to stay focused on exploring new areas in which one's personal expertise can be developed. The Experiencer is more than capable of changing the course of his/her life and finding success in a completely new area of activity.

Line 4

The Experiencer is in danger of straying off the path and losing sight of the way forward. He/she has absolutely no idea how to make progress and is at great risk of getting involved with incompetent and mediocre people. This would have disastrous consequences. The only way forward is to come to grips with the present situation and be completely realistic.

Line 5
The current situation is very beneficial and the Experiencer is going through an important period of personal development. However, the Experiencer is warned that there is a serious risk of being diverted by encounters with people who are absolutely not worthwhile. It is therefore crucial to be steadfast and follow an independent path. In this way the Experiencer will succeed in entering a completely new area of activity and experience personal renewal.

Line 6
The Experiencer has reached a point where a breakthrough can be achieved. Everything is in place and nothing can stand in the way of a lasting solution.

The Shock

The Shock is caused by an unexpected turn of events that has the effect of a wake-up call.

There are two different scenarios in this hexagram.

In the first scenario the Experiencer has been following a wrong course of action. *The Shock* comes when the Experiencer is suddenly confronted with an obstacle that cannot be overcome. This is a completely unexpected failure.

In the second scenario the Experiencer has made the mistake of becoming too complacent. *The Shock* comes when the Experiencer is overtaken by events and is suddenly confronted with a situation that has changed for the worse.

Both scenarios show the Experiencer trying to pick up the pieces after a sudden and completely unexpected twist of fate. This shocking turn of events forces the Experiencer to come to terms with a radically changed reality and find a different way to make progress.

The Shock has a very disorienting effect; the Experiencer may be plunged into a state of confusion and lose all sense of direction. In the midst of this apparent disaster he/she will need to calm down and try to come to terms with what has happened.

It will gradually become clear that this unexpected turn of events is actually a blessing in disguise, a wake-up call, forcing the Experiencer to abandon a mistaken course of action. And then, with an intense feeling of relief, the Experiencer will gladly accept this turn of events and decide to follow a different direction in life. This will open the way towards real progress.

The moving lines

Line 1
An unexpected and shocking turn of events has completely upset the Experiencer's plans. This shock will open the Experiencer's eyes for new possibilities and as a result he/she will be glad to follow an entirely new direction. This will lead to a major accomplishment.

Line 2
As a result of an unexpected turn of events everything is coming to an end. The Experiencer's position is becoming untenable and he/she will have to flee from the situation. This is a shocking experience, but nothing ever lasts in this world. The Experiencer can only hold on to the precious, timeless things that have a truly spiritual quality. He/she will have the power to rebuild or regain what has been lost.

Line 3
A shocking turn of events has left the Experiencer feeling anxious and distressed. The Experiencer should understand that this shock is a wake-up call and means that the time has come to take decisive action. This is the only way to avoid misfortune.

Line 4
An attempt to pursue something which seemed to present a great opportunity has unexpectedly come to nothing. This is a shocking and very disappointing experience. At this point the Experiencer realizes he/she has made a mistake and wasted

time chasing after something that is not really worthwhile. The Experiencer will need a period of reflection to reconsider his/her aims in life.

Line 5
These are turbulent times and the Experiencer has to cope with one shocking event after the other. Nevertheless, the Experiencer is in a strong position and will be able to take the right action at the right time.

Line 6
Things have taken an unexpected turn for the worse. As a result the situation is rapidly sliding downhill. The Experiencer is shocked to discover that he/she is becoming the subject of a nasty gossip campaign. Trying to make progress under these circumstances would lead to misfortune. The time has come to leave the situation before it is too late. .

52

Keeping Still

Keeping Still is the time when action has ceased and everything has come to a halt. It is also the time before action resumes again. *Keeping Still* represents an episode in the Experiencer's life during which it is essential to find detachment from emotional turmoil or bitter disappointment.

Filled with high hopes and enthusiasm the Experiencer has been reaching out to people in pursuit of friendship or a cherished dream. But this has only led to disappointment and failure. All efforts to make progress have ground to a halt and any further effort would only be in vain. Struggling to cope with feelings of frustration and regret, the Experiencer is faced with the prospect of having to find another way forward. This is creating a deep sense of uncertainty about the future.

The Experiencer will need to withdraw and reflect on how to find a way out of this cul-de-sac. Any feelings of defeat or failure should be brushed aside; strength and intent are the only means of dealing with the current reality. It is very important to let go of any emotional involvement in the situation; this is the only way to restore calmness of mind and see things in a clearer, more detached way. Detachment can only be achieved by turning away from all the disappointments and focusing on something else. The Experiencer is not empty-handed and is more than capable of turning his/her attention towards meaningful pursuits that can succeed.

Over time the Experiencer will gradually develop a new sense of purpose and work towards a realistic plan for the future. The Experiencer's intuitive sense of timing will determine when to start probing the outer reality for opportunities. Eventually, these efforts will lead to a complete release from a dead-end situation.

The moving lines

Line 1
The Experiencer is advised to continue in the present situation and resist any desires to move on. This is the only way to avoid making serious mistakes. The Experiencer should use this period to get a clearer idea about his/her purpose in life.

Line 2
It is extremely difficult to take decisive action in this situation, but to simply withdraw is not an option. As a result the Experiencer is becoming disillusioned and confused. Strength and calmness of mind are needed now, because it is crucial to develop a new purpose and regain the momentum in life; otherwise things will just drift on.

Line 3
The Experiencer is urged to find a way to leave the current situation; this is not a place where he/she can flourish. It would be harmful to continue under these circumstances, because the Experiencer's spirit would get crushed in a soul-destroying situation.

Line 4
The Experiencer is trapped in a place where he/she does not belong. The desire to move on is very strong, but the Experiencer should not act impulsively. Calmness of mind and a clear sense of purpose are essential to succeed in finding a new destination.

Line 5
The only way to maintain self-control and avoid making mistakes in this impossible situation is to stop trying to convince obstinate people. The Experiencer is advised to withdraw and concentrate on finding a way to develop beyond the current restrictions.

Line 6
The time has not yet come to leave the situation. There is still some unfinished business in this place; there are important tasks the Experiencer will have to complete before he/she can move on. Over time the Experiencer will overcome regret and be at peace with the situation. He/she will even succeed in having a beneficial influence on others. When everything is accomplished, the way out will open up and the Experiencer will be able to move on.

Working towards a Goal

Working towards a Goal represents the process of making societal progress through developing a strong sense of purpose, identifying a realistic goal, and working towards it step by step. Considerable patience is required for the slow, persevering effort needed to find something that is truly worthwhile.

The Experiencer's present situation will not develop any further and it is becoming crucial to work towards making a transition. None of this will be easy. The Experiencer will have to be prepared to spend a lengthy period of time trying to find the solution he/she needs. This will involve doing systematic research to identify the right solution and then patiently work towards achieving it.

When seeking to make societal progress it will be necessary to follow standard procedures, no matter how tedious or time-consuming they may be. It is also very important to be consistent and correct in all dealings with other people; in this manner the Experiencer will have a positive influence and succeed in making useful contacts.

Above all else, the Experiencer will need to identify a realistic goal, because any efforts to achieve the unattainable will only weaken his/her resolve. Great inner strength will be needed to achieve this goal, but the Experiencer will succeed in the end.

The moving lines

Line 1

The Experiencer's progress is slow and difficult; people can be critical, sometimes unpleasant. Trying to get a foothold as a newcomer is very challenging. Nevertheless, the Experiencer will succeed in setting up home and finding a place in society.

Line 2

The current circumstances are stable and beneficial. Therefore the Experiencer is in a position to make real societal progress.

Line 3

The Experiencer is stubbornly trying to force progress in an area where he/she cannot succeed. Persevering in this direction would only lead into serious difficulties. The Experiencer is strongly advised to strengthen and secure his/her current position, because this will provide an essential vantage point from which to find a new direction in life.

Line 4

The Experiencer's present situation is becoming very unstable and he/she is faced with the challenge of having to find a more secure situation. The Experiencer will succeed in finding a temporary safe haven, but this place will not provide the right circumstances for making longer term progress. It will eventually become necessary to find a place which offers a greater degree of stability.

Line 5

The Experiencer is living in isolation and has been unable to find any recognition. Under these circumstances it is impossible to make any societal progress. The Experiencer will eventually succeed in finding a way out of this predicament, but it will take a long time.

Line 6

The Experiencer will not be able to make any societal progress under the present circumstances. This is not a problem, because he/she can afford to withdraw and follow a path of personal development. Although the Experiencer is no longer directly involved in society, his/her work will be of benefit to others.

54

Transience

Transience represents the ending of a complete cycle in the Experiencer's life. The way of life which has sustained the Experiencer until now is gradually coming to an end. This ending is inevitable and will come of its own accord, leaving the Experiencer powerless to counteract or turn the tide. Any attempts to do so would be futile and could lead to serious difficulties.

This hexagram also represents the absolute necessity to recognize in time the danger signs of a deteriorating situation. Armed with this awareness, the Experiencer will be prepared to step out of a situation that is falling apart before it becomes psychologically harmful.

Any feelings of grief and regret should be put aside. The Experiencer will have to accept that the situation is deteriorating and further progress is no longer possible. Nothing lasts forever. It would be a serious mistake to try to cling to the present situation in the hope that better times will come. By embracing change the Experiencer will be able to escape from a situation that is either rapidly going downhill, or becoming repetitious and pointless.

The Experiencer is challenged to stay strong and constant in times of turbulence and uncertainty, and come to terms with the transient, ever-changing nature of things in this world. The change described in this hexagram presents an opportunity to leave the old behind forever and go on to experience a renewal. In the end, the power of change will galvanize the Experiencer to move on and enter a new phase in life. This will lead to the beginning of a new cycle.

The moving lines

Line 1
The Experiencer has very limited options, but does have enough power to make a significant move. There is an obvious way out of this situation, if the Experiencer is prepared to be realistic.

Line 2
The Experiencer is shocked and very disappointed to discover that he/she has landed in the wrong place with the wrong people. Societal progress is impossible in this situation. The Experiencer is advised to follow an independent path, because there are no possibilities to link up with others at this time.

Line 3
The Experiencer is advised to remain in his/her modest position and wait patiently until an opportunity comes to make progress.

Line 4
An opportunity is presenting itself, but it is not going to provide a lasting solution. The Experiencer is advised to let this one go, because a better opportunity will come up.

Line 5
There is only one opportunity available to make progress at this time. The Experiencer is advised to take it, even though

it is only a modest position with limited prospects. This is the right thing to do, because it will provide a very important social experience.

Line 6
There are absolutely no opportunities for the Experiencer to make progress in this situation. Relations with other people are difficult and are not going to bear fruit. The Experiencer is strongly advised to follow his/her heart and find a way to move on.

55

Abundance

The long brilliant summer seems endless and every precious day unfolds beautifully. It may be the Experiencer has never known such a prolonged period of happiness. He/she has achieved some success and is living in a pleasant, perhaps idyllic situation. Optimism and enthusiasm provide a strong zest for life, strengthening the Experiencer's desire to try to make the present achievement permanent.

The I Ching advises the Experiencer to live this time to the full and be *like the sun at midday,* because the days will slowly become overshadowed by a real concern for the future. The time of *Abundance* does not last; it will inevitably begin to wane. When this happens, there will be a time of sorrow and the Experiencer will have to turn away from a life in a place that is almost fairytale-like in its quality.

As events unfold, the Experiencer will need to make clear, decisive judgments and be prepared to relinquish his/her emotional involvement in the situation. He/she has the clarity of mind to be very realistic and make tough decisions. This will enable the Experiencer to make new plans and move on.

The moving lines

Line 1

In a search for recognition the Experiencer succeeds in meeting a sympathetic person in a high position. They have a good rapport together and everything seems to be very positive. However, this will only be a brief encounter, because it will soon become clear that a longer term involvement with this person would be neither possible nor desirable. Nevertheless, as a result of this encounter the Experiencer will gain an important insight into his/her destiny and be able to change the direction of his/her life.

Line 2

The Experiencer will be unable to find recognition at this time. Any initiatives now would only meet with antipathy and distrust. The Experiencer is strongly advised to hold back and refrain from taking any action. His/her integrity and sincerity will eventually win the trust of others.

Line 3

As a result of a sudden, unfortunate, turn of events the Experiencer discovers that he/she has absolutely no power or influence under the current circumstances. The Experiencer has become completely overshadowed by mediocre people.

Line 4

The Experiencer is living in obscurity and cannot find recognition. In the midst of these difficult circumstances he/she has a surprising encounter with a sympathetic person. Teaming up with this person will enable the Experiencer to make significant progress.

Line 5

The Experiencer finds recognition at last. This is a life-changing event. The Experiencer will be able to radically change his/her way of life and experience great success.

Line 6

The Experiencer has long ago found recognition and success, but is no longer trying to attain or achieve anything new. This way of life only leads to repetition, stagnation and isolation. One never arrives anywhere in this world, because there is no final destination here. Once the Experiencer reaches this insight and understands the implications, he/she will be able to step out of this stale existence and follow a new direction in life.

56

The Wanderer

The Wanderer is the one whose developmental path is inextricably linked to the road, a life of travel and foreign lands. It is the fate of the Wanderer to move from abode to abode, sometimes in sorrow, sometimes in joy.

Wherever the Wanderer goes he/she is a catalyst, a harbinger of change, bringing a fresh and foreign energy into a situation. If there is an injustice, he/she will act as a light or an instrument of cosmic justice and wrongdoers will be revealed. And then the Wanderer will move on.

The Wanderer lives modestly and carefully, often in humble circumstances. Riches and social status are not the property of a person who abandons his/her possessions in favor of the open road. But the Wanderer's life will be rich with experiences. He/she will live in different countries, towns and places and become familiar with all kinds of folk, the languages they speak, and the cultures they belong to. The Wanderer will learn to be fluid and adaptable, both in relation to dealing with people and responding to change.

The Wanderer has the ability to change radically and leave the past behind. As a result he/she can achieve personal renewal, often simply by moving to a new location. Over time the

Wanderer will develop the power to reach penetrating insights into the real meaning and purpose of his/her passage through this world.

The moving lines

Line 1
The Wanderer has found an abode in a location where he/she would like to stay. However, this is very unrealistic, because he/she lacks the means to do so. It would be a great financial struggle to try to continue in this situation, and in the end it would lead to disaster. The Wanderer is urged to see things as they really are and move on.

Line 2
The Wanderer has succeeded in finding an abode in a location where he/she can set up home for a while. Fortunately, the circumstances are beneficial and the Wanderer has enough resources to remain here for the time being. The Wanderer is often a stranger without any friends, but in this situation he/she will find trustworthy people who can be of support and assistance.

Line 3
The Wanderer is at great risk of losing his/her abode. The present circumstances are very trying and the Wanderer is running out of patience with people. However, he/she is urged to be diplomatic and refrain from making hasty judgments. A friendly and cooperative approach will ensure that the Wanderer can remain in his/her abode and continue to receive assistance from trustworthy people. Eventually the right way forward will become clear.

Line 4

The Wanderer has succeeded in finding an abode, but is isolated and unhappy. He/she is experiencing the danger of being a stranger in a strange land. For this reason the Wanderer does not feel safe and is constantly ready to defend him/herself. Nevertheless, the Wanderer will have the strength to hold on in the current situation until a way out can be found.

Line 5

The Wanderer has found a place to settle, but soon discovers that nasty, mediocre people have the upper hand. Trapped in a place of misfortune, the Wanderer realizes that the situation will become unsustainable and starts searching for another place to live. But good fortune is on the horizon. The Wanderer will eventually succeed in establishing him/herself in a new home and start a new life.

Line 6

The Wanderer is strongly warned not to be tempted into making an overambitious move. An impulsive decision could result in a loss of security and material hardship.

57

Penetration

Penetration represents the power of intent, working steadily and patiently to achieve a specific aim. It also heralds a time to honestly examine one's own motives and desires in order to come to grips with the present reality.

The Experiencer will need to closely examine the current situation in order to find out the best way to proceed. There is an important task to fulfill here, but it will require a strong and effective effort on the part of the Experiencer. When the Experiencer sees what has to be done, he/she will be in a position to call in assistance to help complete the work.

There will be opposition, in some form or another, from people with whom the Experiencer is at odds. The Experiencer can adopt a diplomatic approach to try to pacify any opposition, but if this fails, the Experiencer should press on anyway in spite of the opposition.

All in all, the Experiencer will have to make a major effort to work through these difficult and trying circumstances. This will be a daunting task. Nevertheless, this undertaking will succeed; the power of intent can overcome impossible odds.

The moving lines

Line 1
The Experiencer is in doubt and keeps dithering. He/she is urged to focus on gaining a full understanding of the situation. This is the only way the Experiencer will discover how to respond to the current challenges and find a way to make progress.

Line 2
The Experiencer is trying to discover what is blocking his/her progress. To find the answer it will be necessary to penetrate deeply into all aspects of the situation and determine what is actually possible. At the same time the Experiencer will have to thoroughly examine his/her own motives and desires. In this way it will be possible to set a realistic goal and work towards achieving it.

Line 3
The Experiencer has been unable to avoid being drawn into a problematic and stressful situation. It would be a mistake to try to win a victory here, because any further efforts will only lead to exhaustion. If the Experiencer lets go, another way to make progress will open up.

Line 4
The Experiencer is penetrating into the heart of the situation and succeeds in getting a complete picture of the issues at play. Based on this information he/she will be able to avoid getting involved with people who are not worthwhile.

Line 5
The Experiencer has been very robust and succeeded in achieving some reforms in a situation that others have spoiled. Perhaps he/she has been a little too robust, hurting some feelings, but some

people needed to learn the error of their ways. However, the Experiencer should not try to penetrate any further; otherwise he/she will become mired in this situation.

Line 6

The Experiencer should not try to achieve anything more in the present situation, because he/she would come up against deep-rooted problems. Any efforts to make further progress would lead to defeat and exhaust the Experiencer's resources. The Experiencer is strongly advised to seek opportunities for progress elsewhere.

58

The Joyful

The Joyful is paradoxical, because it means both happiness and sadness. It represents enthusiasm and the ability to communicate with others. Sadness comes when joy and enthusiasm can last no longer.

In the time of *The Joyful* people communicate with one another to share their ideas and skills. Communication is the key here, because it opens the way to engage in activity and achieve concrete results. It is a time to step out of isolation and enjoy a positive social experience by becoming part of an enthusiastic team. It will be an intensive, sometimes euphoric experience, affecting and changing the Experiencer in subtle ways. Feeling spiritually refreshed, he/she will be ready to face the future with confidence and optimism.

When the work is finished and the project comes to an end, the Experiencer will take leave and return to the routine of life's daily tasks and whatever pressing business is at hand.

In this hexagram the Experiencer's attitude towards others is of great importance. The Experiencer will need to be friendly and accommodating, but will also need to have strength of character and not be too pliable or overly accommodating; otherwise people will take advantage of the Experiencer's good intentions. On the other hand, if the Experiencer is too hard or inflexible, he/she could seriously damage relations, which would bring the situation to an unfortunate ending. Above all else, the Experiencer will need to have an independent spirit and be prepared to go it alone when the time comes.

The moving lines

Line 1
This is a paradoxical situation. The Experiencer has found some happiness, and for the time being, his/her life is relatively problem free. However, progress is slowly grinding to a halt and the situation is gradually becoming oppressive. During this time the Experiencer will have to depend on his/her inner strength and treasure the good things that can give joy.

Line 2
Things have not worked out, but the Experiencer has not lost his/her deep sense of optimism, which provides the power to keep on going. The Experiencer has the sincerity and the self-confidence to follow the path of destiny and succeed.

Line 3
The situation is deceptive. The Experiencer should not have any illusions that happiness can be found here. On the contrary, this is a trap, in fact, a complete dead end. The Experiencer is strongly advised to grab an opportunity to break out of this entanglement and move on.

Line 4
The Experiencer has found some happiness and contentment, but this is becoming marred by feelings of anxiety and uncertainty. He/she is urged to come to grips with the present difficulties by entering into a dialogue with people who can provide constructive solutions. An agreement can be reached

which will be to everybody's satisfaction.

Line 5
The situation is falling apart, but it would be dangerous to speak out frankly here. The Experiencer's abilities and sincerity are wasted in a place which is dominated by mediocre people. The Experiencer should keep a low profile and find an opportunity to get out.

Line 6
The Experiencer's desire to engage in this situation is very strong. Perhaps he/she really believes that joy can be found here. This would be an illusion; any further involvement would only lead to disappointment. The Experiencer is advised to disengage from the situation and follow an independent path.

Dispersion

In this hexagram the I Ching uses the image of a wooden boat, successfully navigating a passage out of dangerous waters. This illustration serves as a warning to get out of danger.

In an effort to break free from a deteriorating situation the Experiencer sets out on an ambitious plan of action, which seems to offer an attractive solution. The Experiencer devotes a lot of time and energy trying to achieve this solution, but fails to make any progress. As time goes by, the Experiencer's cherished plan starts to unravel, leading to the painful realization that the entire effort has been unrealistic and overambitious. The feeling of disappointment and defeat is almost overwhelming.

At this point the Experiencer should make a major effort to maintain a sense of purpose; otherwise things will really fall apart. Iron determination and willpower are needed to win through and find a solution. The Experiencer simply cannot afford to give up.

In the time of *Dispersion* egoistic ideas and rigid attitudes melt away like ice in the Spring, opening the way for real progress. Letting go of overambitious desires will lead to a more open-minded attitude and a willingness to settle for a compromise.

When the Experiencer is prepared to follow a modest and realistic course of action, the way forward will start to open up and progress will gather pace. The Experiencer will see the wisdom of settling for a more humble solution and succeed in overcoming the present difficulties. This may involve having to leave the situation altogether.

The moving lines

Line 1
The situation is threatening to fall apart. Misunderstandings and secret agendas are having a damaging impact on the Experiencer's position in the organization. The Experiencer will be able to get help to resolve the difficulties and convince people in authority to give their support. Thanks to their assistance the Experiencer will win through in the end.

Line 2
The Experiencer's efforts to make constructive progress in the present situation are failing and relations are falling apart. The only effective course of action is to disengage and withdraw to a safe haven to take stock of things and make new plans.

Line 3
The Experiencer's cherished plans and ideas are not going to succeed. He/she is urged to put them aside and make a realistic assessment of the situation. The Experiencer is in a precarious position and it is becoming increasingly urgent to find a realistic solution.

Line 4
An all-out conflict can be avoided, if the Experiencer lets go of the gains he/she has made in the current situation. This will open the way for better opportunities to make longer term progress.

Line 5

The crisis is reaching a climax; the situation is threatening to fall apart. The Experiencer cries out for help and receives assistance from people in authority. This will resolve the crisis. The Experiencer has made no mistake, but this experience will nevertheless serve as an important lesson.

Line 6

The Experiencer is in a precarious situation, but will be able to stay out of acute danger for now. However, the Experiencer will have to persevere in finding a way to leave the situation, because this is the only way to completely escape from the danger.

60

Limitations

This hexagram represents the absolute limit of what is possible to accomplish. The Experiencer is confronted with conditions and limitations that have a strict, legal basis.

The Experiencer is in negotiations with an established entity, an organization or a private enterprise, in an effort to make a deal. However, in order to reach an agreement the Experiencer will have to consent to a strict set of rules which are legally binding. These rules cannot be changed by the Experiencer; it is the other party who dictates the conditions of the deal. At this point the Experiencer will need to make an assessment of the conditions and decide whether it is worthwhile to accept the deal.

There are two possible scenarios in this hexagram.

In the first scenario the Experiencer decides to pull out of the negotiations, having realized that he/she would be entering into a situation with unacceptable limitations.

In the second scenario the Experiencer decides to accept the conditions of the agreement, even though it would mean having to operate within strict limitations. Although the deal is far from perfect, the Experiencer greatly needs the security the agreement offers.

By graciously accepting the limitations set by the agreement the Experiencer will earn the goodwill of the other party. The Experiencer's correct and consequent attitude will give him/her a certain moral influence. This will make it possible to maintain a modest and secure position, which will prove to be invaluable in the time to come.

A period of stability and relative contentment will follow, but over the longer term the limitations set by the agreement will become too galling to accept. At that point the Experiencer will have to galvanize into action and step out of the confines of a one-sided agreement. This will lead to a major transition.

The moving lines

Line 1
The Experiencer should not try to overcome the current limitations at this time. It would be premature to make any moves now. The Experiencer is urged to take the time to carefully research all possible options and not make any hasty decisions. With patience and perseverance he/she will eventually succeed in breaking free from this confinement.

Line 2
The Experiencer will need to take a major initiative to overcome the current limitations; otherwise he/she will become trapped in an extremely restrictive situation. The time has come to look beyond the present circumstances and search for opportunities elsewhere. The challenge is to look for solutions in a completely new area, putting aside old ideas which no longer have any value.

Line 3
The Experiencer will have to come to terms with the current limitations. There is a real risk of getting into serious difficulties,

if he/she becomes too ambitious. The Experiencer is urged to be realistic and wait for the right opportunity to make progress.

Line 4
The Experiencer is advised to accept the limitations of the situation. By coming to terms with the present reality he/she will be able to team up with others and nevertheless achieve something worthwhile.

Line 5
The Experiencer should accept the limitations of the contract or agreement on offer and not look any further. It provides an opportunity that will prove to be beneficial.

Line 6
The limitations of the situation have become completely unacceptable. It would be a big mistake to try to continue under such restrictive circumstances. The Experiencer will have the power to make a transition, because his/her sincerity will have a positive influence on others and win their support.

61

Trust

This hexagram represents integrity and inner truth. The Experiencer knows what is true and what is not, and has the integrity to uphold the truth.

During this period the integrity of the Experiencer will come under question or be openly challenged. The Experiencer will have to make a sustained effort to convince skeptical people of his/her honesty and good intentions. This will be essential in order to get the necessary support and cooperation to make societal progress.

The Experiencer is sincere and has a thorough understanding of the situation and the important issues at play. This will make it possible to have a positive influence on people and persuade them to resolve the current problems. Gradually, an atmosphere of trust will develop, creating a spirit of cooperation and a willingness to find the right solutions. The Experiencer's open and honest approach will succeed in winning the confidence of even the most doubtful people. As a result the Experiencer will receive all the necessary support and backing needed to make a breakthrough. In the end he/she will experience the joy of accomplishment.

There is also a strong element of justice in this hexagram. It may become urgent to tackle people who are acting against the common good and have been blocking progress. The Experiencer will succeed in revealing the truth about their wrongdoings and justice will be done.

The moving lines

Line 1

If the Experiencer is steadfast in his/her resolve to make a necessary change, and is prepared to go through the first difficult stages, he/she will eventually succeed and make progress. An open and honest approach will win the support of others.

Line 2

The Experiencer's sincerity has the power to influence people who live far away, even though he/she has never met with them. The Experiencer is trustworthy and has a lot to offer; however, in a world of distrust he/she will need to find kindred spirits to get recognition.

Line 3

In an ongoing search for opportunities the Experiencer has been trying to find recognition and success. Unfortunately, the Experiencer has become too dependent on finding worldly success and is constantly swung backward and forward between hope and despair. The Experiencer is urged to stop with these efforts and focus on finding the deeper purpose of his/her life.

Line 4

The Experiencer is advised to break away from the people he/she has been associating with and follow an independent path. This is the only way to avoid serious difficulties or conflict. As a result the Experiencer will be free to follow the path of destiny.

Line 5

The Experiencer is prepared to give up everything in a bid to reveal the truth about the situation. The power of truth will triumph and justice will be done. However, as a consequence the Experiencer's position will become untenable and he/she will have to leave the situation. Nevertheless, this is not a mistake.

Line 6

The Experiencer is not in a position to convince or influence anyone in these circumstances. He/she is urged to come to terms with the very real limitations of the situation. If the Experiencer continues broadcasting his/her opinions, it will lead to serious difficulties.

62

Unrealistic Ambitions

This hexagram represents a major effort to find a place where one can truly thrive. It also warns of the danger of overreaching oneself and running out of resources. The I Ching illustrates this warning by using the imagery of a little bird searching for a place to nest, but it is trying to fly too high and is at risk of becoming exhausted. And likewise, if the Experiencer continues to pursue unrealistic ambitions, the consequences could be disastrous. Success can only be achieved by completely changing one's outlook on life.

The search for a new life in a new place has created a nomadic lifestyle. The Experiencer keeps trying to find a place where he/she can thrive, but every attempt ends in failure and confusion. The desired destination either fails to materialize or succeeds at first, only to end in disappointment. And then the search continues.

Paradoxically, the Experiencer's ongoing quest, which seems futile, is actually essential for the Experiencer's developmental path. It is a journey of increasing self-knowledge and wisdom, rich with experiences, both positive and negative.

In the time of *Unrealistic Ambitions* the Experiencer can successfully deal with the minor problems of everyday life, but any major initiatives or ambitious plans should be put aside until the way forward becomes crystal clear.

During this period the Experiencer will need to come to terms with a deeply disappointing situation that has failed to meet his/her expectations. A painful and difficult process of personal change cannot be avoided. The Experiencer will have to make a major effort to see things in a clearer light, while trying to cope with feelings of regret and disappointment.

Over time the Experiencer will become aware that he/she has been clinging to unrealistic ambitions in the hope of making a success, but has only succeeded in reaching a dead end. This insight will lead to a complete change of outlook and the realization that a new direction must be found. As a result the Experiencer will be able to focus on a realistic goal and pursue aims that are truly worthwhile. A renewed sense of purpose will give the Experiencer the strength and the energy needed to make a transition into a new future.

The moving lines

Line 1
Any attempts to make further gains at this time would lead to failure. The Experiencer does not have the power to pursue any ambitions and will need to concentrate on gaining more clarity to find the right way forward.

Line 2
The Experiencer has very little power or influence. He/she will need to abandon overambitious ideas and aim for a modest solution. This will enable the Experiencer to work towards a longer term purpose.

Line 3
The Experiencer is strongly warned to be extremely cautious

and prepare to counteract a nasty attack from unpleasant and devious people. He/she has very little power, but is in a position to get the support of powerful allies. In this way the Experiencer will succeed in defending his/her interests.

Line 4

The Experiencer is strongly warned to be extremely cautious and resist any temptation to leave the current situation. A misguided move could lead the Experiencer into circumstances in which he/she would be completely powerless. The Experiencer is urged to cease contact with the people he/she has become involved with, because they are absolutely not worthwhile. Everything will eventually fall into place, if the Experiencer is prepared to accept the current reality and remain in the present situation.

Line 5

The Experiencer has been trying to influence the wrong people and will not succeed in making any progress this way. He/she is an outsider without any power or influence and will not be able to find truly sympathetic people at this time.

Line 6

The Experiencer is overambitious and is trying to achieve the impossible. He/she is running the risk of missing out on the only opportunity to find a secure and stable place to live.

63

After the Crossing

After the Crossing represents a time when a major transition has been accomplished and many things have been achieved. However, it will not be possible to maintain this success over the longer term. The situation has reached a peak and is gradually going into decline.

The Experiencer's circumstances are deceptively secure and comfortable, but in reality his/her current success is beginning to wane. Conditions in the Experiencer's living environment are slowly deteriorating and are no longer favorable. Power is now completely in the hands of people whose only priority is self-interest. Over time the Experiencer will find it increasingly difficult to live in a place where selfishness rules. Trying to build relationships in this kind of environment will only leave the Experiencer disillusioned and frustrated. A point will be reached when the Experiencer can no longer engage in positive, meaningful activity and life will just become a daily struggle.

One way or another this situation will end in ruin or disorder, because there is no cohesion between the people, no spirit of mutual regard or cooperation. When things start taking a turn for the worse, the Experiencer will start preparing to make an exit. Seeing the futility of trying to continue under these circumstances, the Experiencer will step out in time and avoid disaster. Thanks to good foresight the Experiencer will be able to make a timely exit and start again elsewhere.

The moving lines

Line 1

In an effort to make progress the Experiencer has come up against obstacles that cannot be overcome. The situation has proven to be more challenging than the Experiencer had expected and he/she is forced to adopt a completely different approach.

Line 2

The Experiencer has become the victim of an injustice and as a result the situation has become unacceptable. It would be a mistake to try to get this injustice redressed. When the time is ripe, an opportunity to make a transition will present itself and the Experiencer will be able to leave the current difficulties behind.

Line 3

The Experiencer has unwittingly transitioned into a situation that is in serious decline. He/she has become trapped in the midst of people who have proven to be worthless. The Experiencer will find that nothing can be done to improve the situation and that he/she will have to look for a completely new direction. Unfortunately, this will become a long and exhausting search, but with strength and perseverance the Experiencer will succeed in the end.

Line 4

The situation is in decline and the Experiencer is faced with the necessity to make a major transition. He/she has sufficient resources to achieve this, but has yet to develop a realistic plan. A radical change of attitude will be needed to develop an effective plan of action.

Line 5

The Experiencer is in a very humble position, in a difficult situation, but has the sincerity and strength of character to win through. The Experiencer will succeed in finding happiness and continue to follow a path of personal development.

Line 6

The Experiencer is trying to find a way to make a transition, but keeps returning to the same old ideas. There is a great risk the Experiencer will exhaust his/her resources pursuing these ineffective ideas. The present situation will remain stable for the time being and the Experiencer should use this opportunity to find a new direction. This is going to require a lot of strength and determination.

64

The Crossing

The Crossing represents an all-out effort to navigate one's way through a tricky situation and eventually make a major transition. The I Ching uses the imagery of a little fox attempting to cross a frozen river; if the ice is too thin or the little fox makes a wrong step, everything will end in disaster.

The Experiencer's desire to make a new start is very strong, but pushing forward without considering the consequences would certainly lead to failure. The Experiencer is in a vulnerable position and therefore it is crucial to avoid taking any risky initiatives. He/she will have to tread carefully; a wrong move could result in serious difficulties or even conflict.

One thing is certain; the necessity to make a transition is real and very urgent, because the current situation is becoming unsustainable. However, the only way to make a successful transition is to find a destination that is truly worthwhile and within reach. Venturing into unknown territory is a risky undertaking and any failed attempts to make a transition will consume the Experiencer's energy and weaken his/her resolve to start anew. On the other hand, if the Experiencer succeeds in making a transition, but arrives in the wrong place, the consequences could be disastrous.

Patience and perseverance are needed now. The Experiencer will be forced to undergo a period of limbo until the time comes to make a crossing from the old into the new. When conditions in the outer world become favorable, the right opportunity to make the crossing will present itself. This will enable the Experiencer to transition to a place where the future will unfold with new opportunities and challenges.

The moving lines

Line 1
As a result of a lack of research and preparation the Experiencer has made a disastrous transition. This has been a serious mistake. The Experiencer has arrived in the wrong place and will now have to find a way to get out.

Line 2
The Experiencer has reached a crucial insight and now realizes why his/her current plans for making a transition will not succeed. This is important progress; it will open the way for a process of elimination which will eventually lead to finding a solution.

Line 3
The Experiencer is warned against trying to score any victories in the current situation; this would only lead to failure. It will not be possible to make any further progress in the present circumstances and the only solution is to make a transition. A new destination will provide the right conditions for significant personal development.

Line 4
This will be an emotionally turbulent period in which the Experiencer will have to go through a difficult learning

process. A vigorous effort will need to be made to undertake a major transition. Self-discipline and strong perseverance will eventually lead to success.

Line 5

The Experiencer should continue in the present situation. With diplomacy and a willingness to reach a compromise he/she will be able to avoid a conflict and have a positive influence on the situation.

Line 6

The Experiencer has succeeded in making a major transition, leaving a dead-end situation behind. The relief is tremendous and the Experiencer celebrates his/her success with great confidence and optimism for the future. However, the Experiencer is warned to be careful and to take nothing for granted.

Epilogue

The I Ching is a numerical compilation of archetypal situations, a book of divination in which numbers are used to access the future. The 64 hexagrams and 384 lines form a numerical system based upon a perfect mathematical model. The I Ching oracle uses numbers to access knowledge from a place where time as we know it does not exist. Numbers are the perfect medium to access what is timeless, because the absolute value of a number never changes and therefore numbers have an eternal value. The magic of the I Ching is its unique combination of eternal numbers and timeless archetypal situations. These archetypal scenarios are independent of time and place, repeating themselves throughout the centuries, generation after generation. This is how the I Ching mirrors the phenomenon of cyclic change in the human world.

This world is an arena in which personal growth and development is the purpose of our existence. The I Ching confirms and outlines this purpose whenever we consult the oracle, acting as a guide to encourage us to walk the path of personal development.

All of the scenarios or archetypal situations, unfolding in the 64 hexagrams of the I Ching, illuminate the developmental path of the individual. An individual following a path of personal development will experience most of the scenarios, described in the 64 hexagrams, during his/her lifetime.

The following two examples illustrate the profound personal development *The Experiencer* goes through on his/her path through the 64 hexagrams. Hexagram 36 *The Darkening of the Light* is a scenario in which the Experiencer has to survive dark times, but nevertheless live through adversity and gain in spiritual strength. Hexagram 29 *The Power of Flowing Water* is a scenario in which the Experiencer finds the strength to forge ahead through challenging and difficult circumstances, all the while gaining in clarity and knowledge.

Consulting the I Ching always reveals the truth about things. The reader is often shown a reality he/she would prefer not to see. When the true reality of a situation becomes revealed, illusions are swept away and there is nowhere to hide from the truth. The I Ching challenges the reader to be prepared to accept the truth about things and act accordingly.

Another difficulty when consulting the I Ching is the time factor. It is impossible to gauge how much time it will take for a divination to come to fulfillment. One may see a tantalizing future unfolding in a divination, but it may take months or years to actually happen. Therefore the I Ching teaches patience and perseverance as the means to achieve an end.

Finally, many of the scenarios in the I Ching show *the Experiencer* struggling to come to terms with change itself. This predicament is often the result of trying to cling to a way of life that is losing its relevance in the reality. A recurring theme throughout the I Ching is the necessity to go through a profound personal change in order to adapt to a changing reality.

In many of the hexagrams *the Experiencer* can be seen clinging to cherished ideas that are no longer of any worth. Sooner or later a point will be reached when the only way to make progress is by getting rid of illusions. This will lead to self-knowledge, and eventually, self-realization.

KEY FOR IDENTIFYING THE HEXAGRAMS

Upper ▶ Lower ▼									◀ Upper ▼ Lower
	1	11	34	5	26	9	14	43	
	12	2	16	8	23	20	35	45	
	25	24	51	3	27	42	21	17	
	6	7	40	29	4	59	64	47	
	33	15	62	39	52	53	56	31	
	44	46	32	48	18	57	50	28	
	13	36	55	63	22	37	30	49	
	10	19	54	60	41	61	38	58	

TABLE OF HEXAGRAMS AND THEIR INNER HEXAGRAMS

Hexagrams	Inner Hexagrams
1. The Creative	1. The Creative
2. The Receptive	2. The Receptive
3. Difficulty in Making a Beginning	23. Collapse
4. Caution and Restraint	24. Return
5. Waiting for Nourishment	38. Discord
6. Conflict	37. The Home
7. The Army	24. Return
8. Unity	23. Collapse
9. The Power of Endurance	38. Discord
10. Treading Correctly	37. The Home
11. Peace	54. Transience
12. Standstill	53. Working towards a Goal
13. Fellowship (Mutual Cooperation)	44. Encounters
14. Great Personal Resources	43. Breakthrough
15. Modesty	40. Deliverance
16. Enthusiasm	39. Obstruction
17. Guided by Events	53. Working towards a Goal
18. Work...Others Have Spoiled	54. Transience
19. Approach	24. Return
20. The View	23. Collapse
21. Making a Judgment	39. Obstruction
22. Authenticity	40. Deliverance
23. Collapse	2. The Receptive
24. Return	2. The Receptive
25. Following the Will of Heaven	53. Working towards a Goal
26. Biding One's Time	54. Transience
27. Seeking Nourishment	2. The Receptive
28. Carrying a Heavy Burden	1. The Creative
29. The Power of Flowing Water	27. Seeking Nourishment
30. Clarity	28. Carrying a Heavy Burden
31. Influence	44. Encounters

Hexagrams	Inner Hexagrams
32. Duration	43. Breakthrough
33. Retreat	44. Encounters
34. Exercising Restraint	43. Breakthrough
35. Progress	39. Obstruction
36. The Darkening of the Light	40. Deliverance
37. The Home	64. The Crossing
38. Discord	63. After the Crossing
39. Obstruction	64. The Crossing
40. Deliverance	63. After the Crossing
41. Decrease	24. Return
42. Increase	23. Collapse
43. Breakthrough	1. The Creative
44. Encounters	1. The Creative
45. Gathering Together	53. Working towards a Goal
46. Authentic Development	54. Transience
47. Exhaustion	37. The Home
48. The Well	38. Discord
49. The Revolution	44. Encounters
50. The Cauldron	43. Breakthrough
51. The Shock	39. Obstruction
52. Keeping Still	40. Deliverance
53. Working towards a Goal	64. The Crossing
54. Transience	63. After the Crossing
55. Abundance	28. Carrying a Heavy Burden
56. The Wanderer	28. Carrying a Heavy Burden
57. Penetration	38. Discord
58. The Joyful	37. The Home
59. Dispersion	27. Seeking Nourishment
60. Limitations	27. Seeking Nourishment
61. Trust	27. Seeking Nourishment
62. Unrealistic Ambitions	28. Carrying a Heavy Burden
63. After the Crossing	64. The Crossing
64. The Crossing	63. After the Crossing

Bibliography

Dening, Sarah. *The Everyday I Ching*. New York: St. Martin's Griffin, 1997.

Douglas, Alfred. *How to Consult the I Ching*. London: Penguin Books, 1972.

Fancourt, William de. *Warp and Weft: In Search of the I Ching*. Milverton, UK: Capall Bann Publishing, 1997.

Hughes, Ernest Richard. *Chinese Philosophy in Classical Times*. London: J.M. Dent & Sons, 1942.

Karcher, Stephen. *How to Use the I Ching*. London: Element Books, 1997.

Lynn, Richard John. *The Classic of Changes: A New Translation of the I Ching as interpreted by Wang Bi*. New York: Columbia University Press, 1994.

Wilhelm, Richard. *The I Ching or Book of Changes*. Translated by Cary F. Baynes. Princeton: Princeton University Press, 1990.

Wilhelm, Richard. *Lectures on the I Ching: Constancy and Change*. Translated from the German by Irene Eber. Princeton: Princeton University Press, 1983.

Authors Biography

Timothy and Johanna Dowdle are an Anglo-Dutch couple who have lived and worked in many different countries and are currently living in the Netherlands. Over the years the authors have studied and practiced the art of divination, using divination as a tool for making important decisions. A red thread running through their lives together has been *The I Ching or Book of Changes*. They first began consulting the I Ching oracle in 1988 and for more than thirty years the I Ching has guided them through many changes, often coaching them through very challenging situations. After returning to the Netherlands in 2011 from a year of intensive social work in the USA the authors decided the time had come to write an I Ching oracle book based upon their own real-life experiences. Their aim is to share the knowledge and wisdom of the I Ching and make it accessible to everyone.

O-BOOKS

SPIRITUALITY

O is a symbol of the world, of oneness and unity; this eye represents knowledge and insight. We publish titles on general spirituality and living a spiritual life. We aim to inform and help you on your own journey in this life.
If you have enjoyed this book, why not tell other readers by posting a review on your preferred book site?

Recent bestsellers from O-Books are:

Heart of Tantric Sex
Diana Richardson
Revealing Eastern secrets of deep love and intimacy to Western couples.
Paperback: 978-1-90381-637-0 ebook: 978-1-84694-637-0

Crystal Prescriptions
The A-Z guide to over 1,200 symptoms and their healing crystals
Judy Hall
The first in the popular series of eight books, this handy little guide is packed as tight as a pill-bottle with crystal remedies for ailments.
Paperback: 978-1-90504-740-6 ebook: 978-1-84694-629-5

Take Me To Truth
Undoing the Ego
Nouk Sanchez, Tomas Vieira
The best-selling step-by-step book on shedding the Ego, using the teachings of *A Course In Miracles*.
Paperback: 978-1-84694-050-7 ebook: 978-1-84694-654-7

The 7 Myths about Love...Actually!
The Journey from your HEAD to the HEART of your SOUL
Mike George
Smashes all the myths about LOVE.
Paperback: 978-1-84694-288-4 ebook: 978-1-84694-682-0

The Holy Spirit's Interpretation of the New Testament
A Course in Understanding and Acceptance
Regina Dawn Akers
Following on from the strength of *A Course In Miracles*, NTI teaches us how to experience the love and oneness of God.
Paperback: 978-1-84694-085-9 ebook: 978-1-78099-083-5

The Message of A Course In Miracles
A translation of the Text in plain language
Elizabeth A. Cronkhite
A translation of *A Course in Miracles* into plain, everyday language for anyone seeking inner peace. The companion volume, *Practicing A Course In Miracles*, offers practical lessons and mentoring.
Paperback: 978-1-84694-319-5 ebook: 978-1-84694-642-4

Your Simple Path
Find Happiness in every step
Ian Tucker
A guide to helping us reconnect with what is really important in
our lives.
Paperback: 978-1-78279-349-6 ebook: 978-1-78279-348-9

365 Days of Wisdom
Daily Messages To Inspire You Through The Year
Dadi Janki
Daily messages which cool the mind, warm the heart and guide
you along your journey.
Paperback: 978-1-84694-863-3 ebook: 978-1-84694-864-0

Body of Wisdom
Women's Spiritual Power and How it Serves
Hilary Hart
Bringing together the dreams and experiences of women across
the world with today's most visionary spiritual teachers.
Paperback: 978-1-78099-696-7 ebook: 978-1-78099-695-0

Dying to Be Free
From Enforced Secrecy to Near Death to True Transformation
Hannah Robinson
After an unexpected accident and near-death experience, Hannah
Robinson found herself radically transforming her life, while a
remarkable new insight altered her relationship with her father, a
practising Catholic priest.
Paperback: 978-1-78535-254-6 ebook: 978-1-78535-255-3

Quantum Bliss

The Quantum Mechanics of Happiness, Abundance, and Health

George S. Mentz

Quantum Bliss is the breakthrough summary of success and spirituality secrets that customers have been waiting for.

Paperback: 978-1-78535-203-4 ebook: 978-1-78535-204-1

The Upside Down Mountain

Mags MacKean

A must-read for anyone weary of chasing success and happiness – one woman's inspirational journey swapping the uphill slog for the downhill slope.

Paperback: 978-1-78535-171-6 ebook: 978-1-78535-172-3

Your Personal Tuning Fork

The Endocrine System

Deborah Bates

Discover your body's health secret, the endocrine system, and 'twang' your way to sustainable health!

Paperback: 978-1-84694-503-8 ebook: 978-1-78099-697-4

Readers of ebooks can buy or view any of these bestsellers by clicking on the live link in the title. Most titles are published in paperback and as an ebook. Paperbacks are available in traditional bookshops. Both print and ebook formats are available online.

Find more titles and sign up to our readers' newsletter at http://www.johnhuntpublishing.com/mind-body-spirit

Follow us on Facebook at https://www.facebook.com/OBooks/ and Twitter at https://twitter.com/obooks